"*This practical book gives you a proven strategy to write and sell an excellent book on any business subject you know and care about.*"

~ Brian Tracy
Author, *The 100 Unbreakable Laws of Business Success*

"*Many people aspire to write a book, but just don't know where to begin. This book is a guide, offering perspective from someone who has written books under his own name and others'. Read this book and put Derek's experience to work for you.*"

~ Skip Prichard
President & CEO, OCLC
former President and CEO, Ingram Content Group

"*No one tells you how hard it is to write a business book. Luckily, Derek's* Bible *makes it easier—much easier.*"

~ Todd Sattersten
Founder, BizBookLab
co-author, *The 100 Best Business Books of All Time*

"*Derek Lewis's* The Business Book Bible *is by far the most comprehensive book I have ever seen on the nuts and bolts of writing a business book. If you're planning to write a business book, then you would do well to read this book first.*"

~ Peter Economy
"The Management Guy" at *Inc.*
bestselling author and ghostwriter of 70+ books, including
Everything I Learned About Life I Learned in Dance Class

"*This excellent book demonstrates why Derek Lewis is a highly trusted authority in the area of crafting powerful, effective business books.*"

~ Michael Levin, *New York Times* best-selling
author and CEO of BusinessGhost.com

"I've taught publishing and self-publishing for years. Because the industry is fragmented, it's hard for a new author to get the information they need all in one place. The Business Book Bible pulls together all of the best information in one cohesive, readable guide. The book is the new business card and your own can help you leverage more business, more speaking, and more media."

~ PENNY C. SANSEVIERI
CEO, AUTHOR MARKETING EXPERTS
ADJUNCT PROFESSOR, NYU

"Don't even start to write a business book until you've read The Business Book Bible. *If you've already started, stop and read Derek Lewis's comprehensive guide. Derek is truly an expert and will answer questions you didn't know you had."*

~ LAURA BROWN, COMMUNICATION CONSULTANT
AUTHOR, *HOW TO WRITE ANYTHING*

"The gold in this book is its comprehensiveness; the material truly lives up to its title. Congratulations! I don't think you missed a single beat. I strongly urge anyone even remotely thinking about penning a business book to start with The Business Book Bible."

~ CLAUDIA SUZANNE
FOUNDER/CEO, WAMBTAC COMMUNICATIONS
FOUNDER/PRESIDENT, GHOSTWRITERS UNITE!
FOUNDER/INSTRUCTOR, GHOSTWRITING PROFESSIONAL DESIGNATION PROGRAM

"If you want to write a business book, you can't afford to miss The Business Book Bible. *Derek Lewis includes dozens of hard-won, actionable tips about writing a great business book. He puts the 'raisins in the muffin.'"*

~ JOHN KADOR
AUTHOR OF *EFFECTIVE APOLOGY*, *THE MANAGER'S BOOK OF QUOTATIONS*, AND OTHER BUSINESS BOOKS

"The Business Book Bible *is informed, approachable, honest and insightful. For anyone writing a business book, whether it's their first or their fiftieth, this is the guide to turn to."*

~ SALLY COLLINGS, BESTSELLING AUTHOR
FOUNDER, RED HILL PUBLISHING

"With a velvet hammer, Lewis begins this book by demolishing every excuse for NOT writing a book. Then, with compelling stories, good humor, and compassionate understanding, he explains how to do it, step-by-step. His focus is business books, but there's plenty of solid advice for any would-be author. His book's closing words are, '...give the world a wonderful book, chock full of things people want to know, presented in a way that delights, entertains, and enthralls'...and Lewis has done just that. Don't write a book without him!"

~ MICHELE DEFILIPPO
OWNER, 1106 DESIGN
AUTHOR, *PUBLISH LIKE THE PROS*

"Engaging. Thorough. Insightful. Thought-provoking. Inspirational. All the characteristics of a typical Derek Lewis-ghostwritten business book in a highly readable how-to volume that generously shares his talents and his hard-won skills with others. Worth taking to work...and to heart."

~ TOM PARKER, WRITING COACH, EDITOR, AWARD-WINNING
NOVELIST AND *NEW YORK TIMES* BESTSELLING GHOSTWRITER

"Everyone has a book in them. Very few people write it. If you have a business-related book hidden in you, you must read Derek's excellent work. It is easy to understand and leads you through, step-by-step. Before you know it, you're done—and it's done right. A must-read."

~ MICHAEL L.F. SLAVIN, WEST POINT '75
FOUNDER AND CEO, U.S. EMERALD ENERGY
AUTHOR, *ONE MILLION IN THE BANK IN 3–7 YEARS*

"The Business Book Bible is a thorough resource that'll save you time, help you get your book started—and finished—and enable you to write a better one."

~ ROBERT SKROB, CPA, CAE
FIVE-TIME AUTHOR, INCLUDING *YOUR ASSOCIATION SHORTCUT*

"I'd like to congratulate Derek on a well-written and thought-out book on how to write your own business book. I suspect it will take the last remaining excuse away from many would-be authors and replace it with a practical guide to writing their first bestseller."

~ DANIELE LIMA
MANAGING DIRECTOR, ROAD SCHOLARS TRAINING & STRATEGIC CONSULTANCY

"*Derek is a gifted ghostwriter. For most people like me, writing is hell. After reading* The Business Book Bible, *I realized it doesn't have to be. The way he approaches the writing process makes it seem natural—even enjoyable. That's why I'm happy to say to any would-be author: YOU NEED THIS BOOK. Derek has done an outstanding job of modeling exactly what he does and putting it into easy-to-use advice. To be honest, he may have done it too well—he's working himself out of a job!*"

~ MATT POLLARD, BUSINESS CONSULTANT, INTERNATIONAL SPEAKER, AND FORMER MANAGING DIRECTOR

"The Business Book Bible *is where every 'wannabe' business author should start. Derek has simply written the best how-to handbook for business authors—full of nuts-and-bolts, commonsense advice on everything from how to write a killer title to the ideal word count. An easy-to-understand blueprint for success that deserves a place on every writer's shelf.*"

~ HOLLY GONZALEZ, COPYWRITER + MARKETING STRATEGIST

"*Extremely well written. Many of Derek's tenets on writing are expressed better than I've ever heard or read anywhere else. There's something inspiring for every writer. I hope he creates much more like this.*"

~ PAUL BOVINO, PLAYWRIGHT, GHOSTWRITER, AND AUTHOR

"*Derek's book is a work of lucidity, intelligence, and compassion, addressing business professionals who want to be authors but haven't a clue how to start. He takes you by the hand, answering questions he knows you have in your head as well as the ones you don't even know you should ask. His warmth and humor interspersed with the technical considerations and insider information make this an easy read. Every entrepreneur or corporate executive can feel in good hands here.*"

~ FRANCINE BREVETTI, GHOSTWRITER AND BOOK COACH AT LEGEND CRAFTER

THE

BUSINESS

BOOK BIBLE

EVERYTHING YOU NEED TO KNOW
TO WRITE A GREAT BUSINESS BOOK

DEREK B. LEWIS

DEREK
LEWIS
INK

Derek Lewis Ink
The Business Book Bible: Everything You Need to Know to Write a Great Business Book
Derek Lewis, M.A.

Published in the United States by Derek Lewis Ink
www.dereklewis.com

ISBNs:
Soft cover: 978-0-9907356-0-1
Hard cover with dust jacket: 978-0-9907356-1-8
Digital: 978-0-9907356-2-5

Cover and interior layout: 1106 Design
Proofreading: Michael LaRocca and 1106 Design

For Mom, who always encouraged me to read.

For Dad, who always encouraged me to write.

CONTENTS

1

AM I READY TO WRITE A BOOK?

"Good writing does not come from fancy word processors or expensive typewriters or special pencils or hand-crafted quill pens. Good writing comes from good thinking."

~ ANN LORING

A LOCAL CELEBRITY ONCE CONTACTED ME because she needed to write her business success story. She was an "accidental entrepreneur": after Hurricane Katrina, she stumbled into an opportunity and was a business owner in her own right before she even realized what was happening. Today, she is a recognizable face around New Orleans and has even garnered international press in her industry.

The impetus for her book was a call from Hollywood. After the success of Louisiana-based reality shows like *Swamp People, Cajun Pawn Stars,* and *Duck Dynasty,* some producer wanted to film yet another one, this time featuring a resourceful Crescent City entrepreneur. Planning to write her book before getting caught up in filming was a good decision. By the time the show finally aired, we could have found a publisher and had the book ready for immediate release. The show could premiere simultaneously with her book hitting the bookshelves. In the end, she decided to go it alone.

When I spoke to her a few months later, she informed me she had bought "The Pen": a gorgeous $1,500 Mont Blanc screw-top fountain pen with which she meant to write her memoir. She laughed about her extravagant indulgence and I ribbed her about it a few times over the call. In the end, though, I again encouraged her to share her inspiring story with the world.

The last time I checked, she had yet to write the first word.

Are you doing the same thing? Do you keep thinking and talking about writing your book without ever beginning? Have you been gathering ideas and stories without ever committing them to paper? Are you trying to figure out what to say before you sit down with a pen?

You will never get your book written until you start writing.

Don't wait. Don't look for someone to give you permission. Don't look for a sign from heaven. Don't wait until you know more or until the stars have aligned. Don't wait until you have read the right book or bought the right pen. Don't wait for anything to begin.

If something in you tells you that you need to write a book—do it.

WHEN SHOULD I BEGIN TO WRITE?

"You must have experience to write a good nonfiction book, so please do not write a book on how to get rich unless you are already rich."
~ PATRICIA CLAY

I received an email from a gentleman in Croatia who asked for help in putting together a book on nutrition and fitness. He wanted to establish himself in the US market via a book first, followed by a business venture later on. He had a great idea. Business books are, hands down, one of the best, fastest, and most cost-effective marketing tools you will ever have. He started off on the right foot.

Too, he had done his homework and identified the US weight loss industry as a lucrative market. Again, he displayed good sense. He even went so far as to profile his ideal demographic and target audience. Kudos for his sensible approach.

The only problem was that he was not an expert in nutrition nor fitness. His experience was nowhere in the area. Not even close. His idea was to hire someone to research enough to write a book on it so that he could claim it as his own.

Now, not every business book is an "expert book" based on the author's expertise in a field. Plenty of great business books have been written by journalists or others who penned a manuscript based on their research and writing skills rather than their own experience. *The Power of Habit* and *A Whole New Mind* stand out as two examples. But before Duhigg and Pink wrote their respective books, they spent hundreds of hours doing their homework first: reading, distilling, cross-referencing, interviewing, arguing, and more reading. Even though they were not the authorities on everything in their books before they actually wrote them, they still had to learn enough to become true experts on the subject matter before they knew enough to write a whole book.

You absolutely should write a book…but you should wait until you know enough to write it.

WHEN SHOULD I BEGIN WRITING? (PART II)

> *"The best way to become acquainted with a subject is to write a book about it."*
> ~ ATTRIBUTED TO BENJAMIN DISRAELI

Check that.

You should wait until you know enough to *publish* it. You should absolutely start writing your book today, even if you don't know enough to release it yet.

One of the best ways to learn a subject is to teach it. Writing takes it to a whole other level. Trying to put a series of cohesive chapters together forces you to learn the topic to a degree you can't imagine until you do it yourself. It forces you to know enough on a subject to—well, to write a book on it.

Client after client of mine tells me that authoring a book about their business helped them reach a new level of understanding. It's not that they did not know their stuff. Most of them were already thought leaders. But[1] having to organize their knowledge into a book and explain it in satisfactory detail made them get quite clear about it.

In a question-and-answer interview with me, my client Greg Short put it this way:

> *The process of writing has been incredibly valuable in helping me think, talk, and deal with these complex concepts at a whole new level. Going into it, I thought I was an expert in the topic area of my book. I came out as an "expert plus one" because of my newfound capability in articulating that knowledge.*

You should wait until you know enough to publish your book, but start writing ASAP.

THE MAGNUM OPUS FALLACY

> *"I have never met an author who was sorry he or she wrote a book. They are only sorry they did not write it sooner."*
> ~ SAM HORN

One of my favorite fiction formats is epic fantasy, such as *The Lord of the Rings*. If J.R.R. Tolkien's publisher had released all three books in just one volume, it would have been massive. It would be too unwieldy,

---

[1] Just in case you hear your high school English teacher in your head, let me reassure you that it is okay to begin a sentence with a conjunction.

resembling a dictionary more than an enjoyable novel. It did not make sense to force the entire story into one book.

By the same token, you do not have to cram everything you know into one massive volume. I've heard more than one author declare that their book will be their magnum opus: the great, all-encompassing work of their lifetime. Your book does not need to be an encyclopedia of everything you know on the subject. It should suffice for the purpose at hand.

Professors with decades of research and study behind them can crown their achievements with a final masterpiece. But business changes so rapidly that a thought leadership book might be out of date in just a few years.

What about the year after you release your book? Don't you think you will have learned a little more? What if the industry shifts or technology renders much of your advice moot? Your masterwork is suddenly insufficient.

This is why textbooks have multiple editions. It is why authors write new books that compete in the marketplace with their older ones. Even business "greats" like Napoleon Hill and Dale Carnegie, whose books have endured for decades and who have inspired legions of followers around the world, released multiple works and editions. It is okay if your book does not contain the depth and breadth of your knowledge.

I wish I could give everyone who wanted to write a book a card with this inscription:

> *Business authors of the world, I hereby give you permission to write more than one book.*

You need not feel as if this book were your final word on all things related to the subject. You have the freedom to write about things that may well be rendered obsolete within just a few years. You hereby have the liberty to write an entire series of books centered on what you know—and you can update them all in a few years—and then sell the new editions, too.

AIM FOR GREATNESS

"You must not come lightly to the blank page."
~ STEPHEN KING, *ON WRITING*

Poppa, my father's father, lived for challenging himself. If he had been a character in a fairytale, he would have been a tinkerer: he was forever creating, inventing, repairing, and improving…well, everything. Welder, mechanic, farmer, fisherman, carpenter, electrician, teacher, merchant marine—he possessed no end of talent.

"But as soon as he realized that he had figured out whatever he was trying to do, he lost interest. Really, he just wanted to see if he could do it in the first place," my dad once told me.

The three barns behind his house (yes, three) held the remains of half-finished and wholly forgotten contraptions, gadgets, and gizmos: two cars, a couple of tractors, a boat, a homemade flame thrower, parts of his CB set, and enough electronic equipment to assemble a working cockpit. He had it all. But his creations sat there, looking almost pitiable.

They had such potential to be great…and yet they were not.

I can say the same about too many business books. They had the seeds of being something truly great. Yet their author stopped short of greatness. They exist, forlorn and forgotten, while the author works on something else. When I read one, I think, *This could have been such a wonderful book…but it's not.*

Books are supposed to be great. Books shape us into who we are. They hold the power to change lives.

✦ *In Search of Excellence* catalyzed the rise of the business book and is largely responsible for the reason I have a vocation today.

✦ *The Art of War* influenced generations of thought, not only in true war but in business as well.

- *The Communist Manifesto* was a catalyst for the rise of socialism in Eastern Europe and forever changed the course of history.

- Napoleon Hill's little gem *Think and Grow Rich* spurred hundreds of thousands of people to work their way towards a better future.

Ideally, millions of people will read your book, right? Then write your book as if millions of people will read it. They will scrutinize it, critique it, digest it, chew it, think on it, and many will believe it. Those who do will act on it, making decisions that affect their careers, businesses, and the eventual outcome of their lives. Take your responsibility as an author seriously.

In five years, I hope I have learned so much that the contents of this book seem almost embarrassing to me. My first ebook was a short little work entitled *How Business Authors Work with Ghostwriters*. Looking back, I am proud to say that, despite its brevity, it is still a good little resource. Whatever it lacked in content, it more than made up for in passion. As a new ghostwriter, my enthusiasm (and good instincts, I might add) shone through. I poured everything I knew into it, plus some of my heart and soul. I did not come lightly to the page.

Your ideas are important. The world needs your book. Put the very best of yourself into your manuscript, and see it through to the finish.

Don't come lightly to the page.

HOW LONG WILL IT TAKE?

> *"I resisted the temptation to rush it out ASAP because I wanted to make sure the paperback was a book worth owning."*
> ~ MARK MCGUINNESS ON HIS BOOK *RESILIENCE*

Listening to an interview, I heard a business guru say that she had locked herself in a hotel room and forced herself to write her latest book over a weekend. I have not read it, but I know one of two things: she either wrote a partial draft or her book is not worth reading.

No one—and I mean but no one—writes a good book in a single weekend.

And if it's not good, why would anyone want to read it?

It takes a lot of work to write your book, both in preparing to do so and in the actual writing, revising, and editing. How long does it actually take? It varies, author by author. If you are an experienced writer of any kind, know exactly what you are going to write about, and already have it precisely structured in your mind, you could start and finish in as little as three months. Some best-selling authors have written their books in even less time. My hat is off to them, as most business authors (myself included) take considerably longer.

If you are a first-time writer, if you are unsure about what your book will eventually look like, and if you do not have all your source material together, it is easily going to take you a year to put your manuscript together. If you were to ask, many would-be authors will confess that they have been working on their book off and on for many years.

But these dates and timelines mask the real issue: once you are finished, will it be a book worth reading? Commit yourself to your book so that years later you can be proud of what you sent out into the world. Your book reflects you: however people perceive your book is how they will perceive you. If your book is brilliant, then by virtue of being the author, you will be seen as brilliant, too. If your book looks lazy, slipshod, and shallow…well, so will you.

Don't worry about how much time you will spend. It is not a race and it is absolutely not a waste of time. Regardless of how long it takes you, the time is going to pass anyway. The question is how you plan to spend it.

ARE YOU READY TO WRITE?

"Writing books is the closest men ever come to childbearing."
~ NORMAN MAILER, *THE NEW YORK TIMES BOOK REVIEW*

Like we discussed at the beginning of this chapter, your book does not begin with a Mont Blanc pen and a Moleskin notebook. It is not conceived on the blank screen of your computer. It starts inside your head—and there is a lot that needs to go on up there before you write the first word.

You have to know how to think about your book. Believe it or not, you have a relationship with your book, as if it were a living, breathing entity of its own. As you delve into it, you will come to love, cherish, and want to throttle it as if it were your own child: unruly, disobedient, wonderful, and inspiring.

Are you ready to invest your time and energy to raise this child? Or are you going to whelp a kid, then ignore it and malnourish it until it emerges into the world a sickly, pale imitation of a human being? Are you ready for the responsibility of creating something wonderful? Are you mentally ready for the hurdles and unexpected challenges it will bring?

The question is really this: are you ready to be a parent?

SOUND BITE SUMMARY

+ You will never get your book written until you start writing.

+ Don't cram everything you know into one book.

+ Writing a book is not a race.

+ Your book is worth doing right.

2

WHAT SHOULD
I KNOW BEFORE
I BEGIN?

*"If my doctor told me I had only six months to live,
I wouldn't brood. I'd type a little faster."*
~ ISAAC ASIMOV

*"Every child is an artist. The challenge is to
remain an artist after you grow up."*
~ PABLO PICASSO

ONE TIME IN A USED BOOKSTORE, I found an old copy of *What Color is Your Parachute?*, the classic career guide that Richard Bolles has updated every year since 1975. One fact that leapt out at me was that most jobs aren't even posted. Bolles pointed out that 80 percent of all filled jobs were never advertised. They are instead filled by word-of-mouth, networking, and serendipity. I have since seen this statistic substantiated by a number of sources, including NPR.

Bolles's takeaway was not that there's a good-ol'-boy network or that "it's not what you know but who you know." Anyone can create these networks by themselves with intention, focus, and hard work. In fact, plenty of people have approached business owners and managers who had been meaning to go through the process of posting the job but did not want to take the time. When the candidate showed up with great credentials and the obvious eagerness to work, the boss hired them on the spot.

Contrast that with an Air Force major I met who had decided not to reenlist. He and his family were living off their savings while he searched for a new career. He proudly informed me that he treated the job search as a job itself, "going to work" at his computer 8:00 a.m. to 5:00 p.m., finding positions posted online, filling out applications, and generally applying for everything remotely related to his skill set.

In other words, "spray and pray": throw a lot of darts in the dark and hope one of them hits something.

While he invested an amazing amount of effort—forty hours a week for months on end, according to him—he misdirected where to invest his time. Less than 10 percent of jobs are filled online, and those positions are usually the low-end kind. So he spent 100 percent of his time competing in the smallest and shallowest end of the employment pool. His core decisions were fundamentally flawed.

It is easy to see his fallacy in black and white here on the page, but are you doing the same thing with your book? Are you so focused on the minutiae such as "Should I use this word or that one?" that you have overlooked the core questions, like "Who is this book for?" Before you begin trying to figure out how to open chapter one, you need to figure out what you're even saying. Who wants to read your book? What should you focus on? What should you include? What should you leave out? I counsel authors to ask these types of hard questions at the beginning of their book. The answers will determine everything else, and even determine the outcome of their book's success.

Many authors want to write their book as quickly as possible and be done with it. But as I will say over and over again: it's worth it to do it right. You have many questions to answer and plenty of work to do. So, take a breath, relax your shoulders, and give yourself some room to breathe.

Before you dive in, let me provide you the five-step process I use to write and ghostwrite multiple books a year. It arose organically from me working with so many different authors and books. I have since discovered that many other writers and ghostwriters use something quite similar.

1. Source material (a.k.a. the discovery phase)
2. Blueprint (a flexible guide to the book's structure)
3. Draft (or, as I like to call it, "Frankendraft")
4. Edit (multiple rounds)
5. Polish

Or, to summarize it in prose: first, figure out what to say. Then figure out how to say it.

You do not need to worry about chapters, transitions, and getting the first sentence "just right" until you are farther along in the process. The first thing is to get everything out of your head and onto the page. Writing a book begins with a brain purge.

The very first question you can ask—and the most important—is, "What's my reader's problem?"

SOLVE A PROBLEM

> *"The number one reason people buy business books*
> *is to find solutions to problems."*
> – JACK COVERT AND TODD SATTERSTEN,
> *THE 100 BEST BUSINESS BOOKS OF ALL TIME*

Year after year, self-help relationship books earn more money than almost all other book categories.

I promise their success does not come from the fact that everyone has a wonderful love life and they just want to know how to tweak it. No, people have relationship problems and they turn to the experts to help them get out of a jam.

People read novels, literature, and even biographies for entertainment. They read business books to solve problems. Few people go to the business section at Barnes and Noble and think, *Oh, that one looks like it'd be a lot of fun. I think I'll buy it.* Your reader does not read books like yours for pure entertainment.[1]

But, like me, they may say, "You know, I do stay cloistered in my office. I think I'll buy this *Talk to Strangers* book. Maybe it'll give me some easy ideas on how to strike up random conversations. Oh, here's *Own the Room*—well who wouldn't want to do that?!"

We buy business books to overcome challenges.

Your own book starts with asking yourself, "What problem does my book solve?" You should be able to answer that question quickly, confidently, and succinctly. I wrote *The Business Book Bible* for people frustrated with writing their book or so bewildered they don't know where to begin.

What about yours? Does your book help people run their business better? That is a good start, but it lacks specificity. What kind of business? Whose business? What aspect of the business?

"My book helps upper managers at mid-sized tech companies create systems that allow their operations to change, grow, and adapt with ease." That is a specific problem with a promising answer. When your prospective reader hears that, they will sit up and take notice: "Hey, this guy's book might be just what we're looking for!"

The more specific of a problem your book solves, the easier it is for someone to recommend it to their friends and colleagues when they go through that problem. The recommender remembers the book that solved their pain and opened their eyes.

---

[1] There are a few nerds and business junkies like me, but we are in the tiny minority.

For instance:

◆ A new startup company needs a short and sweet company culture playbook—that's *Rework* by Jason Fried and David Heinemeier Hansson.

◆ A consultant is having a hard time communicating the value of her intangible services—she needs Harry Beckwith's *Selling the Invisible*.

◆ A busy executive feels overwhelmed and needs help to become more effective—he should read *The One Thing* by Gary Keller.

◆ An entrepreneur faces the crossroads of whether to pursue growth or greatness—*Small Giants* by Bo Burlingham provides wonderful examples of the road less traveled.

Nobody likes to be in pain. When they see your book, they find an immediate way to alleviate that pain. They want it, and it almost does not matter how much it costs. The bigger their problem, the more they want what you sell.

The old saying goes, "Don't be a solution looking for a problem." Before you decide what to write about, decide what problem it solves. Start there, and much of everything else you write will flow naturally from the answer.

HOW LONG SHOULD IT BE?

"There are books of which the backs and covers are by far the best parts."

"I suppose they are those heavy ones, sir," said Oliver.

"Not always those," said the old gentleman. "There are other equally heavy ones, though of a much smaller size."

~ CHARLES DICKENS, *OLIVER TWIST*

The 7 Habits of Highly Effective People is a life-changing book. At least, it was for me. The late Stephen Covey was brilliant. But after so many times hearing his book thud when I put it down on my desk, I had to ask myself the question: did it really need to be that long?

He could have delivered the same degree of insight that he did with a slimmer book. For many, *7 Habits* looks like *War and Peace*: too daunting a task to ever tackle. If his book had been shorter, how many more people would have at least attempted it? How many more people could have had the light bulb moments I did and lived a better life because of it?

On the other hand, what about *Who Moved My Cheese?* Some people would say Spencer Johnson's straightforward idea (and consequently slender volume) was worth the book. But for every one of those fans, I bet you could find four or five others who said, "Twenty bucks for fifty pages? Not happening."

Somewhere between *7 Habits* and *Who Moved My Cheese?* is a happy medium.

A typical business manuscript is about twenty-five thousand to seventy-five thousand words[2] (at the publishing standard of 250 words per standard page, that amounts to 100 to 300 pages). That is a fairly big gap, but when you look at certain books you can see that they are just the size they need to be. Then again, you do not have to look at the page number to know some books are simply too long.

Here are the word counts of some well-known business books, plus a few works of fiction you are probably familiar with for comparison's sake:

+ *Who Moved My Cheese?* by Spencer Johnson: ~10,000[3]

+ *Purple Cow* by Seth Godin: 30,665

+ *Fahrenheit 451* by Ray Bradbury: 46,118

+ The book you hold in your hands: 51,116

---

[2] In the publishing industry, always use the word count to measure the length of a book. Pages do not lend themselves to hard numbers: your printer/publisher may use different margins, different fonts, different font sizes, different spacing after headings, and a number of other factors that influence the final page count. Word count, however, is not so flexible.

[3] I can't find an exact word count, but it's in that neighborhood.

+ *Blink* by Malcolm Gladwell: 70,731

+ *Getting Things Done* by David Allen: 76,858

+ *Nineteen Eighty-Four* by George Orwell: 88,942

+ *The 7 Habits of Highly Effective People* by Stephen Covey: 100,519

+ *The Adventures of Huck Finn* by Mark Twain: 109,571

+ *Atlas Shrugged* by Ayn Rand: 561,996

+ *War and Peace* by Leo Tolstoy: 587,287

Ayn Rand could have easily trimmed her epic novel down by fifty thousand words or more. (As much as I love the book, even I cannot read John Galt's monologue all the way through.) Stephen Covey would have lost little by editing out 10 percent of his book—perhaps even 20 percent. On the other hand, Seth Godin is famous for his brevity, but I would not mind him sharing a few more pearls of wisdom. Steven Pressfield's books on creativity are indispensable, but he is about as succinct as Godin.

Too much is too much, but too little is too little.

A book should be exactly as long as it needs to be. It should not be stretched or restricted to an arbitrary word length. If you can say everything you need to say in twenty-five thousand words, why put in filler material just to pad the word count?[4] If you have groundbreaking theories that necessitate a detailed explanation, why restrict it to sixty thousand because that is what you decided beforehand?

It is true that people judge a book by its heft. Godin's books seem expensive compared to Malcolm Gladwell's because it seems like you get less bang for your buck with Godin. But Seth can get away with writing such short books because of his reputation. Manuscripts with

---

[4] I can relate at least one reason I have heard over and over again: authors believe that the longer their book is, the smarter they will look and the more respect they will earn from others. That works until the first time someone actually reads it and tells everyone about their awful book full of fluff and nonsense.

an academic tilt like Gladwell's have a little more leeway to be thicker because we expect a scholar to be thorough.

Until you establish your reputation, though, you do not have such freedom. You need to stay in the range of twenty-five thousand to seventy-five thousand words. The market likes, expects, and welcomes manuscripts of this size.

(The exception to all of this is if your contract with your publisher specifies a required word count. If you want to be published by a major house, you have to pay the piper.)

Imagine two solid blocks that both measure one cubic foot. The first is made of Styrofoam; the second is made of lead. They may be equal in size, but they are completely unequal in density. The heft is more important than the size.

The weight of your words is more important than the weight of your book.

How Long Should It Be? (Part II)

"They're just stupid numbers."

~ René Johnson

I have experienced firsthand how easy it is to get hung up over the length and word count of your book. I did it with my book *Ghostwriters Write It Better*. As I said, a "respectable" business book has a lower limit of twenty-five thousand words. Even though I knew better, I set that number as my absolute minimum.

At about twenty-two thousand words, I hit a wall. I forced myself to crank out the next three thousand words because I felt that I had to hit that target. I did, though, and the rough draft clocked in at 25,601.

Imagine my resistance, then, when my wife read the manuscript and said, "You know, chapters five and six really say the same thing. You use different stories and different words, but when I summarize the points in my head, you don't say anything different."

I had to catch myself from saying, "But that'll kill my word count!"

She was right. I knew she was right. I knew she was going to say that even before she read it. The stubborn part of me, though, was secretly hoping she would just let it go so I would have an excuse to keep it as it was.

I had fixated on a stupid number.

I went back and combined the two chapters, cutting out about a third of the extraneous material. I did not throw it away (you never throw away good writing), but I removed it from the manuscript. When I read back through the revised version, it said everything it needed to say without beating the reader over the head with repetition. It was a better book for the cut.

And, it was just over twenty-four thousand.

I wanted to stress over those last one thousand words. I really did. I thought, *Surely there are a few places somewhere I can add a few hundred words here and there to hit twenty-five thousand.* Thankfully, my better judgment won out. I could have hit twenty-five thousand, but it would not have added anything substantial to the book. I would be stretching out the material to an arbitrary length and breaking one of my own tenets of good book writing. I simply accepted my imperfect book at twenty-four thousand words.

Before my next edition, I am sure I will have some flashes of insight. Perhaps I will add another chapter or three. But the contents of those chapters will come from true inspiration and deliver real value—not from a psychotic fixation on hitting a certain word count.

They're just stupid numbers.

WHEN THE BOOK BEGINS TO WRITE ITSELF

> "I believe that what we want to write wants to be written."
> ~ JULIA CAMERON, *THE RIGHT TO WRITE*

I have nothing against engineers.

Nearly half of my undergraduate credits came from the College of Engineering and Science. But one day I looked around the classroom and said to myself, *Engineers are a special breed—and I'm not one of them.* I transferred to the College of Administration and Business and never looked back.

I've since forgotten calculus, tensile strength tests, chemistry, and electrical-whatever-that-course-was. But one thing I do remember is Dr. Nelson going through engineering problem-solving skills and saying that one of the best methods was to "go home and sleep on it. In the morning, you'll often know the answer."

The subconscious mind is a mysterious place, doing much of the heavy lifting that the conscious mind can't. It makes connections and opens up new lines of thought that we never considered before. It is one of the most powerful tools available to us—and I believe in making the most of it when it comes to writing books.

After thinking about writing a book for years, your subconscious has had a lot of time to work on it. Much of your book already exists. It is just waiting for you to discover and extract it, as if you were an adventurer looking for long-lost relics, ancient and ageless.

Stephen King puts it like this:

> *My basic belief about the making of stories is that they pretty much make themselves. The job of the writer is to give them a place to grow.... Stories are found things, like fossils in the ground.... The writer's job is to use the tools in his or her toolbox to get as much of each one out of the ground intact as possible.*

Plenty of people find it easy to believe this when writing a novel or even a memoir...but an information-laden business book?

Yes, even business books. They preexist before we write them. Our job is to gingerly get them from dreamland into reality. The better of a job you do, the more clarity you achieve. I tell every one of my authors, "Believe it or not, there comes a time when the book begins to write itself."

All of this sounds crazy to most people. It is like saying that the book is an entity with a will of its own, or that some divine power has predestined the book and is guiding us subconsciously.

It's okay if you don't believe this. When *The New Yorker* interviewer said exactly that to Stephen King, he replied, "That's fine, as long you believe that I believe it."

SOUND BITE SUMMARY

+ Do your homework before you get too far into your book.

+ Five steps: discovery, blueprint, Frankendraft, edit, polish.

+ What's your reader's problem?

+ The weight of your words is more important than the weight of your book.

+ Your book's word count is just a stupid number.

+ Don't write a book too short...but don't write a book too long, either.

+ Your book's already written in your head. Your job is to get it out in one piece.

3

WHO IS MY READER?

"Don't try to visualize the great mass audience. There is no such audience."
~ WILLIAM ZINSSER, *ON WRITING WELL*

STEPHEN KING IS, by any measure, a successful writer. After all, he gave us such classics as *The Shining* and *The Green Mile*. Personally, though, I don't read horror, so I don't like much of what he writes. (However, the *Dark Tower* series was incredible. What a story.)

I doubt he cares. As a multimillionaire, he has more than enough money to shrug off my opinion. More importantly, though, he does not write for me. He writes for people who want to read mass market horror.

I do not like to read John Maxwell, either. While he is a great man with great ideas, his writing style just does not grab me. Obviously, he does not write for me, either. What he says and how he says it ring true for millions of others, though.

If either of these two authors were to change their approach to suit my tastes, they would gain another reader…but perhaps at the cost of hundreds or thousands of others. They cannot and should not write their books to please everyone. They should cater to a certain group of people.

Who is your book for?

Not everyone, I can promise you that.

Small business marketing guru Dan Kennedy's principles can be applied across virtually any industry and any size company (as he has repeatedly demonstrated). He has consulted and created marketing material for more than one Fortune 500 company and countless small businesses. But despite the universal application of his approach, he does not write his books for the big companies. He does not target corporate executives. Wall Street types are not even on his radar.

(In fact, he goes so far as to actively repel them—a counterintuitive and brilliant strategy.)

He writes for small business owners. His target audience is entrepreneurs willing to embrace his unconventional ideas, eschewing traditional marketing approaches and usual corporate thought. But he narrows down his target demographic even further: he aims not only for business owners, but specifically conservative, "capitalism, red in tooth and claw," *Atlas Shrugged*-loving types. He purposefully alienates any number of groups. Yes, he loses out on the potential sales that toning the rhetoric down might bring, but he is fiercely beloved by the tribe who follows him.

Dan knows who his readers are and he writes books just for them, to the exclusion of all others. He must be doing something right: he is the only business author (as far as I know) who has had at least one book (if not more) on bookstores' shelves every year for the last twenty-five years. His readers just can't get enough.

IGNORE EVERYONE ELSE, EVEN IF THEY DON'T IGNORE YOU

> *"I'm not trying to be taken seriously by the East Coast literary establishment. But I'm taken very seriously by the bankers."*
> ‑ JUDITH KRANTZ

In spite of Dan actively repelling people outside of his target market, plenty of other people read his books. Salespeople, west-of-left copywriters, middle managers, truck drivers, job seekers—they all read his books even though they are not written for them and despite the fact that he intentionally insults many of them. His advice is brilliant, so they take the good with the offensive.

Sometimes my authors are worried about losing some people by taking a certain stance or focusing on an issue. The greater risk is watering down your book's content so much that it results in plain Jane vanilla. The better approach is to zero in on who needs your book and write for them. If it is great advice, others will find it.

Made to Stick serves a fairly broad audience. The dust jacket identifies the audience as "people with important ideas—businesspeople, teachers, politicians, journalists, and others…" In other words, people in organizational or thought leadership roles. They are the authors' primary audience. But an important secondary audience might be freelance commercial copywriters who want insight into how to craft the best marketing message for their clients and themselves.

The subtitle of this book—*Everything You Need to Know to Write a Great Business Book*—leaves nothing to the imagination: the book is explicitly for business authors who want to write their business book. No question.

In all honesty, though, people who want to write a book all by themselves are my secondary audience. My real audience is my clients—the people looking for a ghostwriter, editor, coach, or consultant to help them with their book. My tertiary markets include publishers, ghostwriters, and editors who need a resource as they help their respective clients. There may even be a copywriter or two in there somewhere. While I hope to write something that helps them, my aim for this book is to attract people who want to work with me.

This isn't deception. (I just told you, right?) It's simply being smart about leveraging a powerful tool to help you reach your goals.

If the primary audience is your target, the secondary audience is the collateral damage. These are readers who were not looking for this book exactly, but it helps them anyway. For instance, I ghostwrote a "how to do business in _____" country guide. We targeted midlevel managers of multinational companies, but business professors, MBA students, and travelers would also get plenty of use from the book. More importantly, it wouldn't be much of a stretch to market to some of these groups of people. The publisher could send courtesy copies to targeted university departments or specific academics who might see the value in using the book as a textbook or supplement to their classes.

I counsel my authors to not be afraid of excluding some people. When a less-than-ideal reader picks up the book—and if the author has done a thorough enough job speaking directly to their one reader—the secondary readers usually have enough sense to realize it was not intended for them.

Despite that, when they see the great information they can get out of the book, they read it anyway.

What's Your Reader's Name?

"We read to know that we are not alone."
~ William Nicholson, *Shadowlands*

Marketing 101: know your target market.

I find most of my authors have a pretty solid idea of whom they are writing for: managers, front-line salespeople, executives, small business owners, number crunchers. Too many authors do not even get as far as these do. But I also find that their idea of said target market is hazy—a vague collection of impressions, opinions, and personalities.

That's not good enough.

"If only one person in the entire world could read your book," I ask my authors, "who would it be? Don't give me some cute demographic or a marketing stick figure. I need you to identify someone you personally know. Client, old boss, supplier, or colleague, I don't care, but it has to be somebody real. What's their name? What do they look like? Sketch their career history for me. What do they talk about? Do they have kids? Who are they?"

They need a crystal-clear picture of that one person. Doing so helps them to slip inside their reader's shoes and explore what they are looking for in a book. For one, if they are writing a book in a certain field, they should know that field intimately enough to understand the people in it. If they cannot name a single person, then they probably have a lot more homework to do before they are ready to write a book.

This exercise helped one of my authors reorient their book from a general management book (e.g., "This is how the company should approach this issue…") to a specific manager's book (e.g., "This is how the manager should approach this issue—and this is how you, Mr. or Ms. Manager, can personally manage the organizational responsibilities such a task entails…"). The result was a book more focused on how the individual manager handles operations rather than how an organization handles them. In other words, the author wrote the book from the reader's perspective instead of the company's.

Companies don't read books; people do. When you know your reader to the extent that you can see their face and imagine their words, you can write a better book for them. When you are deciding whether or not to include a story or phrase something a certain way, all you have to do is ask yourself whether your reader—your one, solitary reader—would prefer it one way or the other. Instead of writing for a vaguely defined person, you have a clear image in your head of exactly who you are having a conversation with in your book. When a question arises as to whether to include something or not, whether to use one example over another, or to consider what is missing, you can simply ask yourself, "What would the person I know want to read?" If they would be turned off by a certain type of humor, do not include it. If they more readily identify with Jack Welch than Steve Jobs, then by all means, talk about Jack Welch.

This person serves as a proxy for all your potential readers, but don't think of them that way. The person you have named should literally want to read your book. If they do not need it or have already learned what is in it, then it is a good bet that their peers have, too. Write the book they need, in such a way that they want to read it. As long as that ideal reader sufficiently represents the rest of your market, then the book should speak to their situation, solve their problems, and connect with them.

Of course, you need to temper that approach with a bit of common sense. One person can never be the microcosm for your entire demographic. If your one reader has already solved a particular problem, but you know from experience that plenty of others like them haven't yet, then go ahead and include that in your book, too. The purpose of this exercise is to free you from paralyzing indecision and to provide clarity on what you need to write—not limit you to writing one book for a single person.

Despite that, go through the exercise to truly answer the question: if literally one—and only one—person in the entire world could read your book, who would it be?

This necessitates some laser-like focus. It forces you to identify who the major influencer in your field is or who the person who could most affect the outcome of your endeavor might be. With most business authors, the purpose of their book is not to make money off the sales of the book. It is really to use it as a means of establishing their authority, breaking into new fields or client circles, and differentiating them from their competition. With many of my ghostwriting clients, gaining just one new client—and often, just one new sale—will more than pay for the cost of their book. In those cases, they really only need one person to read their book for it to be a success.

Everything after that is gravy.

WHEN YOUR IDEAL READER ISN'T YOUR IDEAL CLIENT

"I never cease to be amazed at the huge number of folks who have valuable information between their ears who don't consider packaging and selling it."
‒ RUSS VON HOELSCHER

Most business authors write a business book because they intend to use it—at least to some degree—as a marketing tool. Ergo, most business authors write their book aimed at their prospective clients.

Let me blow your mind: your ideal reader and your ideal client can be two different people.

I once worked with a group of consultants who provided training for business-to-business sales professionals. Their services were created for frontline salespeople, but their actual clients—that is, the people who made the decisions to use their services in the first place—were the vice-presidents and directors of sales and marketing. The consultants marketed to the senior-level executives who hired them to work with their lower-level employees.

So the conundrum they faced was how to write a book to market to decision-makers while the content of the book was all for those people's employees. What should they do? Write a book to senior executives that underscored the need for such training? Divide the book into sections with some parts for the technicians doing the work and other parts for their respective managers?

The funny thing about authoring a book is that by the virtue of doing so, you are automatically perceived as an expert on the topic. Imagine this: an upper-level executive at a consumer goods giant receives a book—written for business-to-business sales in the retail industry—that wows and amazes him. Did it matter that he was not the explicit audience? Of course not. He is going to hire the authors to train his sales team to do exactly what the consulting group outlined in their book.

The fact that their book exists is enough.

As I've pointed out, the very book in your hands follows the same logic. My explicit audience is people who want to write their business book on their own. My "hidden audience" is prospective ghostwriting clients. But for them, it does not matter that I wrote a book aimed at someone else. All that matters is that they see my experience and expertise, and then hire me to ghostwrite their book on their behalf.

Still yet another client I worked with authored a book aimed at students and newcomers to his particular field in IT. His company's clients would have found little use for the information and advice contained in its pages. Ostensibly, it was worthless to them. But the very fact that he had written a book on his field of expertise automatically set him apart from his competitors. Even if his clients did not read the book he laid down on their desk, the very fact that it existed carried tremendous authority with them.

That's the beauty of a business book: you can write it for one person and market it to someone else.

SOUND BITE SUMMARY

+ Who's your reader? Know their name.

+ Write for your reader. Forget everybody else.

+ You can write your business book for one person and market it to someone else.

4

WHAT SHOULD I WRITE ABOUT?

"Writing is no trouble: you just jot down ideas as they occur to you.
The jotting is simplicity itself—it is the occurring which is difficult."

~ STEPHEN LEACOCK

WOULDN'T IT BE WONDERFUL if we could sit down at the keyboard, begin with "It was a dark and stormy night," and type all the way through to "The End"?

World peace, zero-calorie pizza, and fire-breathing dragons coexist in those same daydreams. Effortless books are a thing of fantasy.

There have been some authors who sit down and bang out a manuscript draft in just a few weeks. They are exceedingly rare. Most of us write in fits and starts, belaboring over what to write and what to leave out.

Forget all that.

Forget about sitting down and typing out a perfect chapter, drafted and edited, ready to show your spouse or friend or colleague. Forget about impressing your old English teacher. Forget about the end result.

Writing a book doesn't begin with writing the book. You must first get your information out of your head and onto the paper. That is, you need to first collect all the raw material for your book. Later, you will turn it into a magnificent manuscript.

So how do you do that?

THE INTERVIEW APPROACH

> *"Wise men speak because they have something to say;*
> *fools, because they have to say something."*
>
> ~ PLATO

As I said in chapter two: writing a book begins with a brain purge.

One place to dump your thoughts is on another person—preferably, someone who wants to listen in the first place.

It is far easier to speak ten thousand words than it is to write them, especially when you have a willing audience. You can gather much of the raw material for your book just from a number of in-depth conversations.

You have any number of options for accomplishing this, from expensive to cheap to virtually free.

On the expensive end, you can hire a professional: a writing coach, a life coach, a developmental editor, or a similar type of professional who has experience drawing an author's rough ideas out. Or, you could go all out and hire a ghostwriter. With my clients, we talk a few times a week for several weeks. We do not have a formal interview process or a rigid structure our conversations must adhere to. They talk about everything they know while I listen. They tell me what they have done with their life, the lessons they have learned, the flashes of insight they have had, how they work, how their business operates, and anything else remotely related to the idea for their book. As they do, I mark interesting subjects or themes that we come back to. After they have exhausted themselves going down a particular line of conversation,

I ask intelligent, probing, open-ended questions that prompt more thoughtful discussion.

Our conversations go all over the place. Sometimes, there is no clear path. With one particular author, we were not even sure what the gist of the book would be until much later. We simply began with him relating one story after another and talking about a truckload of related facts and figures he had culled from a number of articles and sources to validate his advice. Only later, after getting the transcriptions back and looking over all his stories, did we piece together any kind of coherent structure.

If you do not want to spring for a ghostwriter or writing coach, a cost-effective alternative would be to find someone for whom it would be worthwhile to mentor. They should be eager to learn from you and already have an eye towards following in your footsteps. That way, they can ask intelligent questions and help you open up about everything you already know.

One of my coaching clients had a college-age daughter who shared his passion. He recorded their conversations, sent them off to a transcriptionist, and had a chunk of his ideas in writing without ever writing the first word. Similarly, if you have great conversations with a good listener, you should have much of the raw writing for your book. In this kind of arrangement, you have someone who wants to hear about your book pulling your information out of you, you have "paid it forward" by mentoring someone who is eager to receive it, and you wind up with the beginnings of your book. Win-win-win.

Whoever you use, realize that you are committing to several hours of conversation. Therefore, if you go with this option, make sure you work with someone who has that kind of time.

The last, cheapest, and least effective approach is to attempt to interview yourself. Ask yourself questions, while going down the road or sitting in front of your computer, and record your answers. The benefit, besides the cost, is that you know exactly what to ask yourself. The disadvantage is that you already know what you are going to say.

My authors and I inevitably find that speaking to someone is much easier than speaking to no one. With someone on the other end of the phone line, you are forced to put your thoughts, feelings, and ideas into at least the structure of a conversation.

Without someone to hear what you say, you are essentially talking to yourself.

THE PAGE-BY-PAGE APPROACH

"Writing is the art of applying the seat of the pants to the seat of the chair."
~ MARY HEATON VORSE

I do not know why, but when it comes to writing my own material, I find keyboards and computer screens stifling. My best and most original writing comes from me literally writing. That is, sitting down at my "workbench" (a table away from my computer desk) and writing the old fashioned way: with pen and paper.

I promise I am not trying to fit the romantic image of a lonely writer scribbling away at his desk. Retyping everything I wrote into the computer is a pain I would love to avoid. But there is something about writing things by hand that makes my brain work a different way. Ink, paper, and some classical violin playing in the background seem to bring out my most authentic self.

I have a stack of unbound paper (printer paper works fine), a permanent marker, a box of paperclips, and a Pilot G-2 07 gel pen.[1] I grab one piece

---

[1] You can buy expensive pens if you want to. I use these for a few smart reasons. One, they flow smoothly—it is easy to write. Two, they are clickable: I can pull one out of my shirt pocket and be writing in less than a second. Three, I can buy them in bulk—as "America's #1 Selling Gel Pen," you can buy them at the warehouse clubs. Four, since they are so cheap, I can have several everywhere—at my desk, in my laptop bag, by my bedside, and in the car. Five, because they are cheap, I do not have to worry about my wife, children, or friends "borrowing" them—you know as well as I do that, once it is gone, you never see it again. Six, they are ubiquitous enough that I can swipe them from other people and places to replenish my own supply—dwindling, in no small part, because of how many other people swipe mine.

of paper and write a single topic at the top. For example, "Give away the secret sauce," "Balance blatant selling," or "Copyright concerns." Depending on how my mind is working that morning, I may go through a dozen pieces of paper, writing only the main idea at the top of each. When I have exhausted my ideas for different topics or ideas to write about, I quickly search through the different papers until I find one I am ready to write about just then. I start writing in almost stream-of-consciousness; that is, I just write whatever occurs to me about that idea as it comes to mind.

When, in the middle of writing whatever I am writing, another idea or piece of advice occurs to me, I quickly grab another piece of paper, write the idea at the top, and then pick right back up writing the content for the previous topic. That way, I do not lose ideas as they come, but neither do I lose steam as I write about a particular topic.

As you begin to gather ideas like this, you will probably find, as I did, that ideas begin coming more easily. I might find myself checking out at the grocery store and have a flash of an idea. For that reason, I carry a pocket notebook around with me to jot down these random ideas. If I am inspired, I may even write some short paragraphs about it. When I get back to my workbench, I transfer the idea or ideas to their own pieces of paper.

It is in the occurring of ideas that the difficulty lies. Therefore, always be ready to grab those ideas as they float by, forcing them into tangible existence.

I like the neat organization this page-by-page approach allows. I have the freedom to unleash whatever ideas come to mind while I write on a certain idea, and yet each disparate idea is self-contained within its own piece of paper. When I am really inspired, I may write several pages, in which case I just paperclip them together. Again, each topic resides in its own "place," but within that space my musings can roam free.

I do not worry about whether I have a little or a lot. These pieces of paper are not the eventual book; they are just a handy way to get everything out of my head and onto paper without being overwhelmed by the sheer number of ideas going all over the place.

THE BINDER APPROACH

"Don't get it right. Get it written, then get it right."
~ GORAN "GEORGE" MOBERG

I wish I could take credit for coming up with the binder system, but I learned it from the father of self-publishing, Dan Poynter, in his excellent book *Writing Nonfiction*. I would not take the time to explain it to you if it wasn't useful—but it is. I used it for this book and, currently, two others. It works amazingly well.

It is a simple idea: get a binder (like the kind you find at an office supply store) and use it to collect all the material for your manuscript. But instead of it simply being a repository for your ideas, you should make it resemble your book as much as possible. Create a mock-up of your cover (if you want to get fancy, go ahead, but a pencil and crayons will do) and slide it into the cover pocket. Create a spine mock-up with your current working title and slide it into the spine pocket. Write up a draft of what the back of your print book might say and slip that into the back cover pocket.

The inside, too, should look as much like the "real thing" as possible. The beginning pages should have a mock-up title page, mock-up copyright page, and mock-up dedication page. Use loose leaf paper if you want to, but I find the paper tears too easily from all the opening and closing you do with your binder over the several months in use. I would hate to think that some of my earliest and best ideas were lost because they accidentally fell out. Instead, I buy plastic page sleeves. It is a bit more of a hassle, but it works for me.

Dan's binder approach works well with my page-by-page approach. I keep a collection of my topic ideas together in one of the back pockets. When I write some material for that topic, I put it in one of the plastic sleeves and clip that into the binder. At this stage (discovery/brainstorming), I do not try to group the ideas together in any sort of order. For now, the fact that my ideas are on paper and gathered in one place is enough for me.

I am not sure why a physical binder makes a difference. Ostensibly, you could use writing software to keep your ideas in one place, or cobble together some kind of systematic approach of your own on your computer. But if you are like me, you will find that having a tangible representation of the book you are trying to birth will make you think, act, and feel differently.

I remember reading an article one time wherein an IT company—I think it was Hewlett-Packard—let a group of young school age children play around with a visual studio software package. They could paint, draw, manipulate, and create whatever they liked. The researchers noticed that when many of the kids were through, they printed their images out. When the researchers asked them why, the kids pointed to the computer screen and said, "Because it's not real there."

I feel the same way about ebooks. I cannot feel as attached to a digital version as I can to the real thing. Whatever the reasons are for those kids printing their pictures out and me wanting to hold an actual book are probably the same reasons a tangible binder makes us approach our writing project differently.

It makes them real.

WHERE DO I FIND MATERIAL?

"If I have seen further it is by standing on the shoulders of giants."
- SIR ISAAC NEWTON

I have seen the gap on the bookshelves for *The Business Book Bible* for quite some time. But I felt I had to wait until I knew enough before I began writing it. The more I have written, the more I have learned, which is why I now advocate beginning immediately, even if you do not know enough to release it yet. "We write to learn," right?

But what happens when we run out of steam? What happens when it feels like we have written everything we know and yet we see that there are still gaps in the material? Where can we go besides our own heads to find more things to write about?

Believe it or not, you probably still have plenty of material up there—you just need some new tools to help you extract it. For instance, you may not even be aware of some great advice you know.

There are four stages to knowledge:

1. **We don't know that we don't know.** Many of my clients have been from Generation X, and they make a compelling case that they've had to be more adaptive than any other generation before or since. When technology began disrupting business, the generation ahead of them was already senior executives who could get away with not dealing with it. The generation behind them was digital natives. Generation X, however, had to go from telexes to fax machines to email to social media. At first, each of these technologies was a foreign concept to them.

2. **We know that we don't know.** Once they became aware of a technology, they might understand what it did, but they didn't know how to operate it. If someone asked them to fax a document or to check out someone's wall, they'd have no idea what to do. They recognized their limitations.

3. **We know that we know.** After learning how to work each new gizmo, they become adept at not only operating it but dealing with the inevitable bugs, paper jams, and digital snafus that occurred. They were aware of their abilities.

4. **We don't know that we know.** This is the place we strive for: mastery of a craft to the point that it's second nature. I learned to play piano by ear (i.e., being able to play a song from listening to it rather than by note-and-rote). Sometimes my piano teacher would play a groovy riff and I would immediately stop her and

say, "Show me how you did that!" Unfortunately, improvising was so second nature to her that she didn't pay attention to what she was doing. She couldn't consciously repeat it. That's the stage of mastery in which you don't know that you know.

If you know enough to write your book, then plenty of what you know exists in this fourth stage. To bring that buried or invisible knowledge to the fore, you need some external catalysts, like reading someone else's book or attending a related seminar.

If reading something spurs some creative idea of your own, then it's your idea. It doesn't matter that the brilliant fire raging in your mind was sparked from someone else's fire. Through your hard work and focus, you stacked the kindling, it ignited, and you fanned the flames once they sparked to life.

Before I go any further, let me explicitly state that plagiarism is absolutely wrong, destroying both your integrity and that of your book. If you cannot write a decent book without resorting to stealing others' ideas, then you are not ready to release a book.

That said, it is perfectly acceptable to build on top of others' ideas and words. When I hit a wall, I may pick up other books to make me think about other ideas, tips, advice, and topics I could include. For instance, I retell Stephen Covey's story about the professor using rocks and sand to illustrate a lesson on prioritization. I tell it using my own words while giving full credit to Covey as the source of the story (as far as I know).

I learned quite a bit about writing nonfiction books from Dan Poynter and Claudia Suzanne. In fact, much of what I have learned over the course of my life comes from what I've read and people who have invested time in my life. It is inevitable that some of their words, ideas, and approaches to life would wind up in my books.

There is a difference, however, between stealing others' ideas and allowing their ideas to spur your own. I fully credit Dan Poynter with the binder system—but I include it in this book because I have used it myself, not because I needed to beef up my book with more content.

When I wrote *Ghostwriters Write It Better*, for example, I went back through Andrew Crofts's book on ghostwriting. In doing so, I saw several topics I could include in my book. But what wound up in my book were not Crofts's ideas but my perspective and experience on those topics. In other words, reading his book got the gears in my head turning, leading me to write about things on which I had an opinion or advice.

Of course, there are plenty of ideas from others' books that I don't write about, either because they are not relevant to my book, because I have not experienced them for myself, or because I do not have sufficient experience to offer a learned opinion on it.

You can also repurpose stories or news articles. For instance, *The Power of Habit* and *The One Thing* both use a few of the same stories. They did not copy from each other. This was a true coincidence because some of the topics in each overlapped enough that they both delved into the same narrow field of research. Inevitably, they turned up some of the same research studies. They go in different directions, using the same stories to support their respective key points in different ways. They just both use the same studies to do so.

In other words, it is okay to take a story, situation, study, or other external source and then speak to it with your own words. By the time you are finished, you may even find you do not need to include the catalyst in your eventual manuscript. You just needed it temporarily to help you get your ideas out of your head.

REPURPOSING MATERIAL FROM BLOGS AND ELSEWHERE

"Quality business books need planning, structure and research.
If you don't think you can commit the time to do it properly,
I would suggest not doing it at all. You don't want to become
known as 'the guy who wrote that horrendous book!'"
~ VALERIE KHOO, "BUSINESS BOOKS ARE THE NEW BLACK"

I once reviewed a manuscript written by an inspiring author. As I read through his content, though, something keep tugging at the back of my mind. The book had obviously been written by the same guy all the way through, but at the same time it felt like there was someone else behind the book, too. It was not as if two different people had contributed content, but as if the one author could not make up his mind. The differences were subtle but prevalent.

Then, finally, it dawned on me: the content was all assembled from his blog posts over the years. The subtle differences I intuited were reflections of his growth as a person and writer over that span of time.

He had a great story and insightful advice. Unfortunately, he hid it behind the rough draft of a manuscript. He fell prey to the idea that he could copy-paste his blog into Microsoft Word and *presto!*—instantly have a book. He let his enthusiasm overrule his good sense. Unfortunately, it showed.

A blog makes an excellent source of ideas and inspiration for your book. I would absolutely draw from it, if you have one. But it cannot be used as is. I would not even use it cleaned up. After writing so many posts and having so much more time to dwell on your ideas and further flesh them out, surely you can come up with something better that can be woven into a harmonious whole in your book rather than stick out like a sore thumb. Surely you have had more refined ideas and learned how to write better since you posted that blog months or years ago.

I have a similar stance on talking your book out. My friend John Spence used dictation software to "write" his last book and his forthcoming one. He can get away with that because he is organized and speaks in a style that naturally lends itself to a good book structure. Two, he had good help from his publisher cleaning the manuscript up. It works for him, but his example comes with a "folks, don't try this at home" warning label. (Too, he had already written a book before he began using dictation software.) Again, transcripts can be a great source of raw material, but do not use them as the polished finish.

Similarly, if you turn your transcripts straight into a book, then you should be able to take a book and turn it into a transcript, right? You should be able to climb on stage or begin a teleconference and effectively serve your audience by just reading straight from your book, shouldn't you? No.

We can usually tell when a speaker is reading from their notes or speaking naturally, even with our eyes closed. Talking and writing are two different media for communication, and they are not perfectly interchangeable. While you can use one as the basis of the other, the creation of one is not the creation of the other. The same goes for white papers, case studies, marketing brochures, sales copy, interviews, reviews, or anything anywhere else. They can be the genesis of some part of your book, but you cannot copy-paste them straight in.

The one and only time I have seen something close to an original blog or transcript used as the basis of a good book is *The Republic of Tea*. The authors used their dozens of back-and-forth faxes (this, before the days of email) as the bulk of their manuscript. There is enough magic in their exchange that it makes for an enchanting journey of the genesis of a wonderful business. The book works because of a confluence of factors: magic, narrative, and editorial help. However, if you read the acknowledgments, you'll see that there was a quite a team of people involved in its editing and polishing.

To be blunt, there are no shortcuts in writing a good book, so do not waste your time trying to find them.

WRITE MORE THAN YOU NEED

> *"The greatest danger for most of us is not that our aim is too high and we miss it, but that it is too low and we reach it."*
> ~ ATTRIBUTED TO KEN ROBINSON, *THE ELEMENT*

In Stephen King's book *On Writing*—which is perhaps one of the best books on what it really takes to be a writer—he said one of the best lessons he ever learned came from a local newspaper editor he worked with while a high school student. In the margins of a rough draft he submitted, the newspaper editor simply wrote: "Second draft = 1st draft – 10%."

Write more than you need.

When you get to the editing and perfecting stages, you will cut out extraneous material, find duplicate ideas and points, and condense longwinded explanations. By beginning with plenty of meat, you can trim the fat. Too many authors, though, discover that even after exhausting themselves, their content is still insufficient. In the discovery and drafting stages, don't be afraid of putting in too much.

It's easier to prune it than pad it.

SOUND BITE SUMMARY

+ There's more than one way to get your book out of your head. Use them all.

+ "Get it written, then get it right." – Goran "George" Moberg

+ There are no shortcuts to a good book.

+ It's easier to prune your writing than to pad it.

5

HOW DO I
STRUCTURE
MY BOOK?

"I love being a writer. What I can't stand is the paperwork."
~ PETER DEVRIES

IN CHAPTER FOUR, instead of sitting down to write your book, you went on an expedition to recover the fragments scattered around the forest of your mind. When you emerged from that jungle, you had armfuls of relics.

But those relics are in bits and pieces. They do not resemble the *objet d'art* that will eventually be your book. So how do you get from here to there?

I used to tell my authors that step two in the writing process was to write an outline of the book. These days, I clarify that by saying step two is to write a "working" outline of the book—really, a blueprint. "Outline" sounds so concrete and definitive, and this phase of the project is anything but. A blueprint helps you keep in mind that you know what you're building, but you still have room to change things as the project progresses.

To have your blueprint in hand requires organizing the chaotic mess you have in your book binder. (That is, if you took my advice in chapter four.) After several weeks or even months of accumulating ideas, resources, papers, articles, facts, figures, and stories, your binder should be pretty thick. By the time it is, you may even be growing disheartened at the idea of trying to tame the beast that has become your book.

Where do you even begin to uncover the manuscript-to-be under all that tangled mess?

THE TAMING OF THE SHEAFS

"The most exciting phrase to hear in science—the one that heralds new discoveries—is not 'Eureka!' but 'That's funny...'"

~ ATTRIBUTED TO ISAAC ASIMOV

First, type all of your handwritten notes. I am sure you could find a service provider (or even an eighth grader) who could do this for you, but I find it helpful to go back through each of my meandering thoughts. Sometimes it sparks another thought or gives me a chance to flesh out that one a little more.

Then, print it all out[1], gather everything you have—your musings, scraps of paper, articles you have collected, pictures, and anything

---

[1] Yes, writing is paper-intensive and many cringe at the thought of using a ream of paper or two in the process. However, I can make an argument that trying to conserve paper in the writing process is a moot point:

1. If you write a book that no one reads, then you wasted all the paper you used to print all of your books anyway. When you consider that, wasting some extra paper in the planning stage is a comparatively tiny sacrifice.

2. I read plenty of books that are way too long. If the author had done a better job in the organizing stage, they could have saved hundreds, if not thousands, of extra pieces of paper in printing copies of a book that should have been shorter in the first place.

3. While I am an advocate of being responsible for the resources with which we are blessed, I am also an advocate of practicality—if you want to conserve our natural resources, there are many smarter ways you can do that than by saving a few scraps of paper.

else—grab a pair of scissors, a magic marker, and some paperclips, and go find a place where you can spread out. I use our queen-size guest bed, but the living room floor will do in a pinch.

Pick up the first piece of paper and ask yourself, "What is this about? What questions does it answer? What topic does it speak to?" Scrawl the broad idea at the top and then set it down as the first of what will become a stack of papers.

Pick up the next page. If it can be broadly grouped into the same category of idea, then it goes with the first piece of paper. Otherwise, it starts its own new stack. Don't worry about getting it perfect—just decide on something for now because you will almost certainly change it later. Let that paper start a new stack. Then go to the next one. If it can be grouped with the first or second stack, great. If not, it starts a third one. Page by page, they all go in their own respective stacks.

As you go through, you may see that one stack could be combined with another if you just broadened the respective topics. Alternately, you may see that you could divide one pile into two if you just broke down the big idea into two smaller ones. Some of your stacks may have only one piece of paper. Some of your papers (especially stories or ancillary information) may not fit into any neat stacks.

If you find that the top half of a page should go in one stack and the bottom half in another, cut them up and place the pieces where they belong. I have even cut out individual paragraphs, splicing the remaining two pieces of paper together because they flowed while the offending paragraph belonged elsewhere.

Now, looking at the assorted piles scattered across the bed and other nearby surfaces, you can see what you have to work with (literally). For me, the relatively thick stacks usually become their own chapters. The sparse stacks are sometimes combined with other stacks, or I may chuck them altogether. It is hard to not include some great thoughts or a neat story, but if it just doesn't fit—well, it just doesn't fit. I save it, put it aside, and make peace with the fact that my book does not have to be a veritable encyclopedia on the subject.

I am breezing through this task here, but the reality is maddening: *Should I really devote an entire chapter to this idea? Do these few sheets of paper represent everything I know about that? What about all these pieces of paper that don't fit anywhere? Surely I can't get rid of all of them!*

As you have witnessed just in this book's pages, authoring a book is not an exact science. Your stacks of paper will likely be an organized mess. But that is the essence of discovering your book: you chip and chip away, revealing more and more of it, until it is uncovered in all its glory. You may have a eureka moment where the stars suddenly align, the heavens open up, the angels sing, and the essence of your book gingerly wafts down in all its celestial glory. More likely, though, finding the keystone idea or new thread will be like those guys in the lab: "That's funny…"

You will notice that you have a disproportionate amount of thought on one subject or that the original premise of your book is a bit light on substance. You may come across a sentence that you scribbled down before bed one night and realize that it describes your real idea.

If a general organization does not naturally emerge from this exercise, you may need to play with a different organization, or you may need to go back to the discovery phase to get some more content down. If that is the case, then put in the time. Don't try to win the Super Bowl with only half of your team on the field.

Barring a substantial lack of content, though, your raw material should self-organize into the suggestion of a book outline. It is okay if one stack is a hundred times bigger than another or if one stack consists of just one sheet of paper. The important thing is to get a grasp of the potential flow of information. You can pare it down or beef it up later. Right now, you're still trying to get a handle on your overall book.

The good news is that this is not the last time you will visit the idea of how to structure your book. You may be in the middle of your second draft and experience a flash of brilliance. Do not look at this step as casting your manuscript in stone. It is simply another round of shaping, molding, and sculpting your ideas. Do it enough times and you will eventually have your own David.

See What's Not There

"Discontent is the first step in the progress of a man or a nation."
~ Oscar Wilde, *A Woman of No Importance*

Once you have your raw material somewhat organized, you have to take a long, hard look at what you have—and what you are missing. One of most difficult things about this step is not only seeing what is there, but seeing what is not there. Are there logical gaps in your content? Are there big questions your reader would expect answered?

You have to make sure that you have said everything you wanted and/or needed to say. Go back to the problem your book solves. Is it still the same problem? Are you still writing for the same audience? Has your premise changed in any way?

Regardless of the answers, you need to go through a round of comparing the content you have against the needs of the reader. Your focus must be tight; your insights, dead on; their attention, hooked.

The Undergirding Structure

"I'm only a novelist on occasion. Many of my books are made up of brief texts collected together, short stories, or else they are books that have an overall structure but are composed of various texts."
~ Italo Calvino

You have a number of different models you can use to structure your manuscript. I will tell you about the two I most often see and use in business books.

The first is what I think of as the linear approach or the "logical argument." Some authors' content naturally lends itself to this structure. Chip Conley's *Peak* and *The 7 Habits* are linear, progressive books that reflect a certain methodology or approach. As such, most consultants' processes usually follow this model. The idea is that there is a natural step-by-step logic that undergirds the manuscript and thus requires a linear, step-by-step presentation of the material.

The other popular structure is what I think of as the "facet approach." Instead of a sequential presentation of ideas and facts, the author's content shows how the idea can be applied in a number of situations or how a theme continually crops up in different areas. *Influence* or *Made to Stick* come to mind. I picture a diamond where the viewer can only see one side at a time. As the reader progresses through the book, the author slowly turns the diamond so that the reader sees a new facet of the gem (the author's main idea or premise), but the gem itself does not change; only the reader's perspective on it. In many cases, it does not really matter which side the reader sees first or in what order the cuts are shown; they exist independent of each other. The whole is beautiful, but the viewer does not need the context of the other sides to appreciate the beauty of one facet.

As I related earlier, with one client I ghostwrote a "how to do business in" for the author's country of expertise. He wanted to talk about business opportunities, culture, dealing with the government, and more such advice people needed to know. At the outset, such a jumble of information did not lend itself to any kind of flow. But once we wrapped our heads around the idea of a facet approach—that all this information was really just different aspects of being a successful business professional in that country—we relaxed and enjoyed the process. We did shuffle the chapters so they began with the macro and eventually narrowed down to the micro, but that was really for the reading experience rather than the necessary flow of material.

In *Get off Your Attitude!*, each of Ryan Lowe's chapters was different aspects of how a positive attitude can change that area of your life: finances, faith, giving, career, friends, and more. While his life story was interspersed throughout the book, it was not presented in order. As such, the final order of the chapters was not critical. He had an order that felt right to him.

You can mix and match as needed. There are no real rules for how a book must be structured or best flow. For instance, your book may have three sections that each express a different aspect of your idea, but within each section you may build a logical argument. Or, you might group your idea's facets under broad headings or overarching topics just to lend a certain degree of organization to it.

OVERARCHING THEMES

"The formula [for a business bestseller] seems to be: keep the sentences short, the wisdom homespun and the typography aggressive; offer lots of anecdotes, relevant or not; and put an animal in the title—gorillas, fish and purple cows are in vogue this year."
- *THE ECONOMIST,* "HOW 51 GORILLAS CAN MAKE YOU SERIOUSLY RICH"

This quote appears in an article that pokes fun at business books while bemoaning how astonishingly bad most of the genre is. But the writer unwittingly picked up on a great piece of advice: have a mental anchor for your reader to come back to. An overarching theme grounds them and guides them through this new territory.

Your ongoing idea is the glue that holds all the various pieces of your book together. It does not have to be something that crops up in every section or necessarily every chapter. It just needs to periodically appear to give your reader a sense of cohesiveness. In a handful of my clients' books, we created a fictitious story to illustrate how the respective authors' processes played out in real life. That way, the reader did not get lost in the minutiae of their methodology.

The oft-used and equally oft-ridiculed metaphor is also an option, as in *Who Moved My Cheese?* But *Cheese* is really a business fable, like Patrick Lencioni's excellent books (*Getting Naked* is one of my favorite business book reads ever). These are really narratives with an underlying business theme (vs. a business book that uses some narrative, like I often do with my authors).

Your theme could also be a bit less tangible. In *The Small-Mart Revolution*, Michael Shuman used a stream of examples of local business owners who successfully competed against Big Box retailers. The implied overarching theme is that of David and Goliath.

Then, of course, some books have their big idea automatically in the content itself. A story of business success, personal or corporate, is an ongoing narrative. No need to reinvent the wheel there.

Plenty of business books do not have an overarching theme and do just fine. Virtually none of Tom Peters's books nor Jim Collins's do. While the title of *What Color Is Your Parachute?* is a clever allusion to a metaphor, the book itself does not have a recurring theme. These books present the author's advice without an anchor, and yet they've hit multiple bestseller lists.

Regardless of how you incorporate this idea, it needs to serve the greater purpose as a framework, anchor, or roadmap. The idea is to give your reader an easy way to categorize and keep track of what you present—a mental map, if you will, so they can easily categorize new pieces of information as you present them.

In *The Billion Dollar Paperclip*, my author used a theme as simple as a paperclip to hold all of his disparate ideas together and give his readers something to continually loop back to.

Your theme should arise organically out of your material. If you have to force it onto your manuscript, then stop. It should weave in and out of your chapters, blending seamlessly—not stick out like some aftermarket modification.

Now, Write Your Blueprint

> *"In preparing for battle I have always found that plans are useless, but planning is indispensable."*
> ~ President Dwight D. Eisenhower

Some writers and ghostwriters get incredibly specific with bulleted outlines that clearly state the point of not only each chapter section but each paragraph.

On one hand, I admire these overachievers' efforts. That takes a lot of energy. On the other hand, I feel sorry for their significant other: I think that level of neurotic detail points to some deeper issues that they should probably discuss with a trained professional.

My outlines are more about clarifying what I have already discovered than completely laying the groundwork for further writing. They begin with a high-level summary of the manuscript's details. What are the author's ultimate goals? What is the book's structure? What is the central theme or main takeaway, i.e. the big idea? Who is the reader? What problem of theirs does the book solve? What is the one-sentence summary of the book? What are the working title and subtitle? These kinds of details reorient me to the core elements of the manuscript, especially after hunkering down in the weeds for weeks on end.

Then, I go one step further in and write a high-level summary for each chapter. What is the chapter's working title? What's the main takeaway? What is the one-paragraph summary of the main takeaway? How does it tie into the big idea? What stories, anecdotes, examples, and analogies do we plan to use to illustrate the primary points?

As you can see, my book blueprints are really just summaries of what I figured out in the taming of the sheafs and what has been rolling around in the back of my mind.

You cannot view your outline as a set-in-stone, gospel blueprint. It is a working document that clarifies your thinking and your efforts. If you get halfway into your first draft and have a flash of brilliance, then ditch the outline. Write a new one. Then get into your second round of revisions and discover another insight.

First-time authors are understandably nervous. Unsure of their book's eventual success, they wish the process were straightforward, structured, and concrete. They want the reliability of knowing what's to come; they want to see the end from the beginning.

Alas and alack, my friend, the Muse is not so predictable: creating is inherently chaotic.

SOUND BITE SUMMARY

- ✦ Don't start writing your book by writing your book.

- ✦ Don't be afraid to look beyond yourself for inspiration—but only after you're tapped out.

- ✦ There are no shortcuts to writing a good book.

- ✦ Write more than you need.

- ✦ First, figure out what to say. Then, figure out how to say it.

6

How Do I Write My First Draft?

"Most people don't want to write a book. They want to have written a book."
~ Unknown

GHOSTWRITE IN CHUNKS.

From discovery sessions with my authors and from the blueprint, I know what should go in chapter one. Drawing from those two main resources, I create a chunk of writing around an idea. When I hit a stopping point or run out of material, I skip a few lines and move on to the next idea. I do not worry about tying those two chunks together. Since I may later discover that the order of the ideas presented should be rearranged, it really does not matter if two pieces work together or not.

It can always be smoothed over later.

Sometimes when I get finished "chunking" a chapter out, it does not even read like a proper first draft. It is more like a Frankenstein monster of a draft. Like Igor, I gather bits, parts, and pieces from all over the place with no idea how they will work together in the end. I just get them on the table first. The brilliant flash of lightning that brings it to life comes later. The important thing is that I have a working draft comprising all the major points for that chapter. I set it aside and allow it to simmer in the back of my mind while I move on. Chunk by chunk, I draft another chapter, set it aside, and start on the next one.

The idea here is to not get hung up on getting it "right." You are creating the building blocks that you need to construct your book. Just like real building blocks, they can be rearranged, restacked, and reassembled in any way you please. (This is true even of individual sentences. I have often found that a paragraph could be substantially improved not by rewriting it, but simply by moving a couple of sentences around.)

While this process will take a lot of time, it should steadily move along since you already have the seeds of your ideas and a general blueprint for your book as a guide.

So now, after spending hours getting your knowledge out of your head, putting serious thought into organizing it, and hammering out the potential structure, you finally start working on the first draft of your book.

CHAPTER ONE

"Begin every story in the middle. The reader doesn't care how it begins, he wants to get on with it."
~ Louis L'Amour

A great novel often has an unforgettable first chapter—even an unforgettable first page. When you get hooked in the first few paragraphs, you want to read the rest. Either because of the humor, the intrigue, or the startling insights, the beginning sets your expectations high.

One of my all-time favorite books, *The Hitchhiker's Guide to the Galaxy*, begins with:

Far out in the uncharted backwaters of the unfashionable end of the Western Spiral arm of the Galaxy lies a small unregarded yellow sun.

Orbiting this at a distance of roughly ninety-eight million miles is an utterly insignificant little blue-green planet whose ape-descended life forms are so amazingly primitive that they still think digital watches are a pretty neat idea.

If you can make me laugh in the first two sentences of your book, you have a reader who will stay with you for the rest of the ride.

The Tiger's Wife, a magical tale that suspends you between reality and disbelief, begins like this:

The forty days of the soul begin on the morning after death. That first night, before its forty days begin, the soul lies still against sweated-on pillows and watches the living fold the hands and close the eyes, choke the room with smoke and silence to keep the new soul from the doors and the windows and the cracks in the floor so that it does not run out of the house like a river. The living know that, at daybreak, the soul will leave them and make its way to the places of its past—the schools and dormitories of its youth, army barracks and tenements, houses razed to the ground and rebuilt, places that recall love and guilt, difficulties and unbridled happiness, optimism and ecstasy, memories of grace meaningless to anyone else—and sometimes this journey will carry it so far for so long that it will forget to come back.

The author begins the novel in this spellbinding way, and the spell remains unbroken through the rest of her book.

In both cases, I was captivated, even if it was for entirely different reasons. The respective authors set an irresistible hook on the very first page and reeled me in until the very end.

Business authors often miss this altogether. Perhaps they are so in love with their insights, so close to their ideas, or so wrapped up in their own world that they forget their reader does not live there with them. They rush to present their arguments and advice, overlooking a crucial detail: their reader has not decided to read the whole book yet.

They bought it and they may start it, but that does not mean they have firmly committed themselves to finishing it.

Too, your book competes for their ongoing attention. Time constraints, boredom, focus, a new project, another book promising to solve their problems—it's easy to lose your reader's interest. If you do not grab it upfront, odds are they will put your book down and never pick it up again.

According to one source, you have only eighteen pages to truly capture your reader's interest. That's right—eighteen. Now, it may be that your information is so compelling that your content captivates them, much like water to a man in the desert. Hopefully, you have written a book for a market so hungry that they will devour whatever you set before them. The more common scenario, though, is writing a book for people who are

1. busy
2. skeptical
3. in need of entertainment

If you can write your book in such a way that it's as interesting as it is informative, then you have a much better chance of keeping your reader engaged.

After eighteen pages, that's it. Either they'll finish your book or it will sit on their bookshelf...on their nightstand...in a box...for years, never to be picked up again.

In school and college, we are taught to begin an analysis by stating and defining the problem. That's fine advice if you want to get an A in the class. But business books are different. If your title and cover copy are clear, then your reader picked up your book because it offered a solution to their problem. Ergo, you do not need to spend chapter one talking about the problem; they are probably neck-deep in it already.

Too, I find that many authors who have a methodology or process like to link their steps to chapters, especially if their process has enough steps that they can keep them synchronous: step one in chapter one, step two in chapter two, ending with step seven in chapter seven. While the parallelism soothes their neuroses, it disorients the reader by diving right into the content without preparing the reader for what's to come.

For most business books, chapter one should be like the beginning of a James Bond movie: enough to whet your appetite before coming to the necessary evil of the title credits.

If you do not fulfill the expectations of the reader, capture their interest, and earn their trust and respect, you will probably lose them altogether. If they never read all—or even most—of your book, then they will never reap the full benefit. This, of course, means you will never reap the full reward for having written it in the first place.

Chapter one is really about setting the stage. It's about giving people enough so that they make up their minds that they're not going to leave after intermission.

Make those eighteen pages count.

PUTTING IT ALL UP FRONT

"The secret isn't in the ingredients. It's in the cook."
~ JOY LEWIS

The author of one business advice book[1] tells a fantastic story. It is an all-American rags-to-riches story. In the first chapter, the author relates how as a young boy he saved enough money to buy his single mother an armchair so she could finally sit down after work—the first new piece of furniture she had ever owned.

---

[1] Title and author purposely withheld—not because I ghosted his book, but because I am slightly criticizing it. One of my tenets of being a professional is to be gracious. For me, that means avoiding embarrassing someone when I am criticizing their work.

Talk about turning on the waterworks.

The first two chapters were great. He took me on a personal journey of overcoming incredible obstacles with a crowning achievement of owning a chain of niche stores each grossing over a million dollars—a first for his industry. He set the bait, and I swallowed hook, line, and sinker. Unfortunately for me, that was as good as it got.

Immediately after chapter two, the book switched from me strolling through the author's life into him giving straightforward advice: "Do this. Don't do that. Definitely don't do *that*." He interspersed some examples and anecdotes here and there, but the remainder of the book simply did not have the fiery passion that so enthralled me in the first two chapters.

My guess was that the author wrote the first two chapters himself, got stuck after writing some of the rest, and hired someone else to quickly finish the manuscript for him. After a little internet sleuthing, I found out I was right about the writer-for-hire, and I am fairly certain I have the different parts of the book pegged correctly.

A business book—or any book, for that matter—should pack a punch upfront, but the rest of the book needs to follow that lead. In this case, the ghostwriter should have worked with the author to pull more stories out of him. Then, as a team, they could have used some of the great content from the first two chapters to spread throughout the book. They did not need to space it evenly or formulaically[2], but if they had peppered stories around the whole book instead of packing it all upfront, the book would have been so much better. As it was, I got excited at the beginning, but then my interest waned and, by the end, fizzled out completely.

He provided sound business advice, clearly established his credibility, and delivered on the promise of the book. The book still turned out okay…but it could have been so much more.

---

[2] Yes, I had to look that up to make sure it was a word.

OPENINGS

"Make your readers want to cheer your name or make them want
to tear you limb from limb, but never let them be bored."
~ ERIC RHOADS

Not only should your book start with a hook—every chapter (and, if you can manage it, every subheaded section) should start with one, too.

It doesn't have to be something complex and involved. It simply needs to capture the reader's attention; something that says, "PAY ATTENTION!" Start with the climax of a dramatic story and work backwards. State a shocking statistic. Ask a provocative question. Relate a cheesy story about your childhood. Take a controversial position.

The beginning of every chapter should draw you in, just like a good novel. Your curiosity should be piqued, your interest aroused, and your attention captured. If each chapter can pull you in on the first few lines and set the hook, chances are that you will read just a little bit farther— just to see what happens.

POINT OF VIEW AND TONE

"Only kings, presidents, editors, and people with
tapeworms have the right to use the editorial 'we.'"
~ MARK TWAIN

Maybe it's because I'm an American, but the British monarchy's use of the "royal we" seems weird. I mean, when I speak in the third person ("Derek thinks that's funny!"), people around me get unnerved. When I speak in first person plural ("We think that's funny!"), people around me freak out.

For some reason, though, it is socially acceptable for us to write in any of the persons: first, second, or third. When you start writing a business book, you get to choose whichever one you want.

The first person (i.e., "I," "me," and "we") is best for autobiographies and other one-sided stories. That is, books where only one person is present. If it makes it any easier to remember, you could call it the "one-person" because there's only one person narrating the story.

The third person (i.e., "he," "she," "they," and "it"[3]) works for biographies or where the author necessarily needs to remove themself. The third person used to be *de rigueur* for research-based and academic books. Thankfully for the rest of us, the industry has moved away from this. (I mean, can you imagine how dry Daniel Pink's and Malcolm Gladwell's books would be if they adhered to this archaic rule?)

By far, most business books use that wonderful narrative voice that most closely resembles everyday speech: the second person (i.e., there are two people present: you and me). That's what this book is written in. It lets me, the author, speak directly to you, the reader. I don't have to pretend that I'm not here, as I would with the third person, nor do I have to pretend that you're not here, as I would with the first person.

But the narrative voice is a separate issue from the tone of your book. Some books are conversational and even humorous. Some are conversational yet straightforward. Some are downright cold.

To a degree, the tone of your book needs to match your reader's expectations. If you work for a consultancy dealing with financial markets, then a personable, down-home style may not work for your audience.[4] If your book empathizes with your reader's plight, then a one-on-one approach makes sense.

My best advice: write naturally. If you know enough to write a business book, then you have probably already picked up on your market's language and preferred style of being addressed. Your instincts should guide you.

---

[3] Not to mention "one," as in, "If one were to apply oneself, one would find one's efforts paying off…" Ugh.

[4] But even then, I like to take William Zinsser's advice: "Just because people work for an institution, they don't have to write like one. Institutions can be warmed up. Administrators can be turned into human beings. Information can be imparted clearly and without pomposity."

Whatever your choice, the key is consistency. If you use the second person, then stick with the second person. If you begin in the first person in chapter one, you cannot suddenly address your reader in chapter three. If you're going to pretend they're not there, then pretend the whole time.[5]

FRAME YOUR IDEAS WITH AUTHORITY

"You are the storyteller of your own life, and you can create your own legend or not."
~ ISABEL ALLENDE

Joshua Bell is perhaps the most gifted violin virtuoso in modern history. A prodigy from the age of three, he has captured the hearts and minds of music lovers all over the world, from European royalty to fans of *The Red Violin*. With grace, he plays the most difficult pieces ever composed on a $3.7 million, 1713 Stradivarius. Tickets easily sell upwards of a hundred bucks a pop and he often plays to a packed house. Many in the audience feel privileged for the opportunity to even witness such artistry in their own lifetime.

So why, then, did a Friday in January find Joshua Bell, clad in jeans and a baseball cap, playing his Strad in a D.C. Metro station at rush hour?

The Washington Post wanted to conduct a social experiment: place a world-renowned artist in an ordinary setting to see if everyday people recognized extraordinary greatness. If D.C. is representative of humanity at large, we failed miserably: out of the 1,093 people who rushed past during the forty-three minutes he played, only 27 dropped any money (he earned a whopping thirty-two dollars), and a disheartening total of 7 people actually stopped to listen.

---

[5] Consistency is also the secret to writing a book with multiple authors. Choose either the second-person plural (i.e., "We suggest you do this…" and "We saw that…") or the third person (i.e., "The team thought this…" and "They did that…") and stay with that narrative voice throughout the entirety of your book. There are few things more disruptive and grammatically sinful than switching points of view.

Why?

For one, people were on their way to work. When I was an employee, I had to get my daughter ready for school, drop her off, and punch the clock before my draconian boss docked my pay. On my way to work, the only things I stopped for were red lights and old people. Everything else got mowed down.

Understandably, if a government bureaucrat recognized Bell's playing as something uniquely beautiful, the hustle and bustle of their life may not have permitted them the space to fully appreciate what was happening in that singular moment.

The journalist who arranged and reported on Bell's experience offers a better explanation, though: context.

People were rushing through their daily lives and had no frame for the breathtaking artistry going on not four feet from them. Some of whom the journalist talked to later reported that they never even heard the sounds of the violin, much less paid attention. Others said they thought his playing sounded like "generic classical music, the kind the ship's band was playing in *Titanic* before the iceberg."

Plenty of marketing and psychology studies address how the lack of context alters a person's perspective. One of my favorite studies was of two groups of people who sampled five, twenty, and one hundred dollar wines. The group who could see the price tags overwhelmingly chose the one hundred dollar wine, even in anonymous responses where their peers couldn't see their choice.

Blindfolded, though, people overwhelmingly chose the twenty dollar bottle.

Seeing the one hundred dollar price tag literally changed the way people experienced the wine: when they expected one wine to taste better than another, it did.

When people are informed that they are about to hear one of the most skilled artists of our time, who then comes onto the stage of the performing arts building, clad in a tuxedo, to the thundering applause of hundreds of respectable people—well, they sit up and take notice.

They expect Joshua Bell to be extraordinary because they have been conditioned to believe he is such. They have a context within which to place his performance.

You, as a business author, must accomplish the same feat. You have to provide people a frame in which to place the expertise you provide. Without educating them on who and what you are, they may never appreciate the genius that is at their fingertips.

You have just a few pages to convince your reader that the book they hold in their hands is worth their time and attention. If you do not provide the right context for what they are reading, though, you face an uphill battle. You must establish your expertise, win their respect, earn their trust, and seize their attention, all in a short span of time.

As I said earlier, some authors take an academic approach to structuring their book: chapter one—state the problem; chapter two—define the problem; etc. But because they did not properly condition their reader to hear the advice from the world's leading expert on the topic, what reasons does that reader have to heed them? The book might have been written by just another hack trying to make a name for themselves.

Some authors fear they will be perceived as bragging. In a speech or in everyday conversation, yes, the same words might be construed as bragging. But a book is a unique medium. Subtle, artful demonstrations of your accomplishments and recognitions are expected and necessary. Letting your reader know that they can trust your advice because you have achieved A, B, and C is a service to them. You want to help them move from across the table—where their defenses are up and their filters are in place—to your side of the table, where they look forward to hearing what you have to share. They can relax and soak up your wisdom, knowing they are in the hands of a master, instead of doubting and arguing every point you make.

You believe your content is valuable (why else write a book?), but it is your job to make sure your reader perceives it as such. You can do this by presenting your achievements, who your clients are, what circles you run in, what degrees you have, the experiences you have had, and whatever else points to your credibility. When you impress your reader upfront, they take the rest of what you say more seriously.

You do not have to brag. That is, frankly, a crass and clumsy way to achieve this. If you do it right, it does not feel that you are trying to impress your reader. Rather, it feels like you're having a conversation while the reader draws certain assumptions based on the context of your information. That way, they arrive at the conclusion that you are impressive on their own—and people always trust their own conclusions more than they trust yours. Show; don't tell.

Your reader wants to trust you—give them a reason to.

THE SECRET SAUCE

> *"Don't worry about people stealing an idea; if it's original,*
> *you'll have to shove it down their throats."*
> ~ HOWARD AIKEN

I remember reviewing a manuscript for a publisher representing a successful Texan entrepreneur. In addition to his many ventures, the man also ran a coaching business. Throughout the book, he alluded to the information he provided in his coaching classes without explicitly providing it, as if he were teasing the reader. In my list of recommendations to the publisher, I suggested that the author's book could provide the best value possible by providing the most value possible.

For example, you might imagine that I am shooting myself in the foot by writing this book. After all, if someone else can write their business book on their own, what would they need a ghostwriter for? Ergo, the best strategy would be to use this book to demonstrate my prowess and impress my potential clients without actually telling them how to do it for themselves.

The first problem with that approach is that it is based on fear. The premise is that there is a limited supply of potential clients. The more who know how to write a book on their own, the less they will need me.

While that is logically true, I like to live in a mentality of abundance. I know that if I ghosted a hundred books a year for the next century, I still would not dent the demand of people who need, want, and are willing to pay for my help. I do not live in fear that my book's sales will cannibalize my other business sales. That's laughable.

The second thing wrong with that idea is that it simply ignores the fact that regardless of knowledge, it's useless without the skills to implement it. A Spanish teacher should not be worried about students taking her job just because they bought the textbook. Despite them having the same knowledge she does, they do not have the mastery of skill necessary to do her job. While I certainly hope this book helps many people write their own book, I know plenty will still need my help in some shape, form, or fashion.

Third, it violates the implicit promise an author makes to their reader. If my book's marketing implies that I'm going to show you how to write a business book then, by Joseph, I am going to show you how. Imagine how distrustful you would be if you had bought this book to discover that I was not, in fact, willing to share my trade secrets but instead used the entire book to pitch my other products and services. If I do not deliver on the promise of this book, how can you trust me with anything else you buy? A book is a marketing tool—but it is not only a marketing tool. It has to deliver serious value to its readers. Otherwise, you are a fraud.

Fourth and finally, experience and observation show that the opposite is true: the more you know and show, the more business you will reap. Tom Peters certainly holds nothing back in his books, and yet is still paid huge sums of money to come tell company teams what they could read for themselves. Marketing guru Dan Kennedy has written some two dozen books, all of which contain profound pearls of wisdom, and yet still has plenty of ideas left for the rest of his marketing and coaching businesses. My client who authored a book on a specialty of international law isn't worried about clients not needing them. Quite the opposite: their book demonstrates just how much their clients do not know, thereby underscoring their incredible expertise.

If I ever had any doubt that this fourth point was true, it was soundly put to rest after a childbirth class. With the upcoming birth of our second child, we hired doula René Johnson to be with us at the birth. We also took advantage of the childbirth course she taught, despite having to give up four hours every morning for three Saturdays in a row. I joked with my wife that, after that much class, I should be ready to be a doula myself.

I soon discovered just how dumb I was.

I was astounded by how much I didn't know. Since my wife was nearly finished with her master's as a certified nurse midwife, following several years as a labor and delivery nurse, I thought I had absorbed enough info to at least get through the birth of our second child.

After just the first class, I was absolutely convinced that we could not have our son without René. She absolutely, positively had to be there. My respect for her knowledge was multiplied and my evident ignorance firmly established.

You see, even after instructing me in an intimate seminar for twelve hours, giving away all the practices, techniques, and knowledge she had, the result was not that I was ready to steal her business. No, I realized how desperately we needed her.

I relate this story to encourage you not to be stingy with your reader. There may be times you find it prudent to withhold certain pieces of information (the exact compound for the miracle drug you created, perhaps), but these instances are few and far between. Even McDonald's finally revealed the ingredients of its own "secret sauce." Despite the recipe now being public knowledge, McDonald's profits haven't been hurt. In fact, the company freely shows everyone, competitors and franchisees alike, its secret: systems. The burger joint routinely takes hormone-driven, gum-smacking teenagers off the street, gives them a few basic instructions, and achieves consistent quality (I use that term loosely) across all its restaurants, from Vancouver to Venice to Veracruz.

Often imitated but never duplicated, McDonald's real secret sauce is standardized execution.

Said another way: if the success of your business is based on something that can be written on a few sheets of paper, then you don't have much of a business, do you?

TELL A STORY

> *"We don't need a list of rights and wrongs, tables of dos and*
> *don'ts; we need books, time, and silence. 'Thou shalt not' is*
> *soon forgotten, but 'Once upon a time' lasts forever."*
> ~ PHILIP PULLMAN

History has forgotten more than you or I will ever know. Facts and records have been lost to the ages. Entire cities lie buried somewhere, never to be remembered. But do you know what has survived the fall of Troy, the sack of Rome, and the destruction of Pompeii?

Stories.

Cinderella was old when I was a kid, yet the story still enchants my daughter and makes Disney a gazillion dollars a year. Aesop's fables date back to the beginning of Western civilization, and yet they're still in print. All major religions rely heavily on parables and stories.

Academia traditionally favors facts, hard data, and solid research over stories, folklore, and anecdotal evidence. As well they should: I don't want to take medicine based on some old wives' tale about how it cures warts and wrinkles at the same time. But many business authors write in an academic style: intelligent, obfuscated, theoretical, and stilted. Why? Perhaps because they crave the respect of the academic community, they were taught in formal universities, or they fear no one will read their work otherwise. If your book is intended only for professors used to that, then you might want to follow in these authors' footsteps.

Well…no, not even then.

Like I said earlier, you want your reader to connect with you, the author. Keeping your book all theory with no stories makes you seem like the mighty professor. While you may certainly demonstrate your authority, would your students want to approach you during your office hours for help? As the all-knowing business author, you may be accorded respect, but will potential clients follow up and hire you to help them with their problems?

To put it succinctly:

Information	Stories
Boring	Interesting
Impersonal	Intimate
Informs	Compels

Let me show you the difference between these two extremes, conveniently within the same book. In *Man's Search for Meaning,* Viktor Frankl recounts surviving the horrors of four Nazi concentration camps, including Auschwitz and Dachau, only because of his belief that despite his tragic plight, his life still had meaning. As a psychiatrist before the war, Frankl had begun to form his own theories about what motivated mankind, but his prolonged torture and harsh life under constant threat of death put his ideas to the test. He decided he could either live what he had preached or turn his back on everything he had believed up to then. Thankfully for the rest of us, he chose life.

Frankl divided *Man's Search for Meaning* into two parts. The first recounts his experiences from his first imprisonment until the day of his liberation. The second half of his book explains his own psychiatric school of thought, logotherapy, in which he states that people aren't truly searching for pleasure (as Freud believed) or power (as Adler believed) but for a purpose—a goal worth living for. The first half of his book is primarily his story, with some commentary sprinkled throughout; the second half is primarily an explanation of logotherapy.

Guess which part is riveting and which isn't?

People don't like information; we like stories. We want to read about Frankl's hopes and dreams, and how he found a reason to go on even while bruised, starving, and forced to live like an animal. We want to read about the beauty he saw in the Bavarian mountains and a stormy sunset while slogging through the snow with swollen feet to build a railroad. We want to feel compassion for him as he watched his father die or after he returned home to find that his wife didn't survive the camps.

After being swept up in so many emotions, we suddenly find ourselves in a drab lecture hall, hearing a professor drone on about logotherapy and transcendental existentialism. Being a dime-store psychologist myself, I enjoy the subject, but I don't want to read a minitextbook on it.

Half the reason to write a business book is to provide information. You must accomplish that purpose. But the other half is to form a relationship with your reader. They do not want to be taken on a tour of a new place with a disembodied narrator pointing out the sights. No, they want a flesh-and-blood storyteller sitting beside them—someone with bad breath and freckles and a pulse. They want to connect with someone real.

Your reader won't connect with your information; they'll connect with your stories. They can't connect with an absent narrator; they can only connect with a person.

"People don't care how much you know until they know how much you care." It's a cliché, but the powerful idea behind it is that people don't trust your words until they trust you. That's why it's so crucial to inject personal insights, personal stories, and personal anecdotes. Once we understand where you're coming from—what's shaped your worldviews, what experiences you've been through—we can buy into what you're saying. Once we get past our mistrust of you, we can listen to your words.

Your book does not necessarily need to be all stories. Depending on your reader and topic, that may be too "fluffy," lacking in real substance. But you can intersperse anecdotes or real-life examples throughout. You could think of them as the salt that makes the main fare more palatable; the sugar to help the medicine go down.

I'm not talking about dumbing it down. I'm talking about making it accessible. Make it easy for your words and ideas to easily flow for your reader.

What kinds of stories?

Any kind. Use personal examples from your childhood. Talk about what you saw on Oprah. Cite an example from Arabian history. Quote something you read in *Oliver Twist*. Discuss a blog post that raised your eyebrow. Create or repurpose an analogy. Borrow ideas from unrelated industries or hobbies. Make up a hypothetical scenario.

People do not connect with information. They connect with stories. I cannot close a phone book before forgetting the number (literally; I can't remember a random sequence of numbers), and yet I remember the story of how Stanley Marcus created a "sundae" for a Neiman-Marcus shopper from a fish bowl, layers of multicolored sweaters, and a ruby for the cherry. This, after more than a decade since reading *Minding the Store*.[6]

"But MY readers are different. MY readers are sophisticated CEOs of huge companies, not some machine shop workers in Texas. MY readers are educated. MY readers don't want to be entertained. MY readers don't have a sense of humor. MY readers are German."

Yes, I'm sure some of your readers are workaholic automatons with no personality and no desire for anything but the facts. These people don't read business books. They read only boring academic journals of the driest subjects and eat little children for breakfast.

These are not your readers.

Your readers are flesh and blood humans. As much as we would like to believe that we are rational creatures, the fact is that we make

---

[6] At the Biedenharn Museum in Monroe, Louisiana, I once encountered a lady who had actually been present as Stanley Marcus created said sundae. I felt like a piece of history came alive for me, instantly searing Stanley Marcus into my memory forever. This is a silly example, but it is a serious illustration of how including stories in your book can tie a reader to your book on an emotional level.

most decisions on an emotional level first, and only then use our rational mind to justify our subconscious decisions.[7]

While your story does not need to be a tearjerker, the fact that it is about a person makes it personal—and when it's personal, it is, to a degree, emotional. Therefore, it connects with your reader on an emotional level—a far deeper connection than you could ever make by engaging solely with their conscious, rational mind.

USING STORIES, ANECDOTES, AND EXAMPLES

"Write about small, self-contained incidents that are still vivid in your memory…Think small and you'll wind up finding the big themes."
~ WILLIAM ZINSSER, ON WRITING WELL

"The truth matters, to be sure, but so do the many versions of the truth, which can offer just as much insight."
~ JEFFREY ROTHFEDER, MCILHENNY'S GOLD

Don't give me an abstract principle and expect me to figure out how to apply it. Give me a specific example and trust that I'm smart enough to extrapolate.

That statement itself is a generality, so let me give you a specific example.

Lee LeFever leads the team behind some of the best informative content on the web. With videos, his company makes ideas easily accessible to us common folks. His impressive client roster includes Google, Dropbox, Intel, and—the stuff of my childhood dreams—LEGO.

In chapter one of Lee's book *The Art of Explanation*, he tells the story of his forty-five-year-old friend, Trevor, who had begun running again after his doctor recommended more exercise. However, he was falling short of his goal of preparing for a half-marathon. A friend suggested

---

[7] For excellent reading on how we make decisions on a subconscious level, I suggest *Blink, A Whole New Mind, The Power of Habit, Made to Stick,* and *Signal vs. Noise.*

he try changing how he actually ran. It had never occurred to Trevor to examine how he ran—that there was an art and skill to it.

As Lee recounted, "He learned about proper posture, stride, and how a foot strikes the surface, and discovered tactics that professional runners use to stay healthy."

Lee's book smartly uses a concrete story to introduce the basic idea behind his book. But instead of relating the general ideas Trevor learned, I wish Lee had been ultraspecific. I don't need Trevor's entire exercise routine, but I would have liked to know exactly what he did differently. Did he make an effort to make sure he landed on the ball of his foot instead of his toes? Did he shift his center of gravity while running? Did he perform different exercises to limber up? Did he lengthen or shorten his strides?

Because Lee does not give at least one detailed example of what his friend changed, I found myself wondering just exactly what he did. As the author, Lee does not want my mind wondering and wandering. He did a great job of arousing my curiosity; he just needed to finish the job.

You would think that by giving a generality, people could individually draw lessons from the thirty-thousand-foot level down to where they lived. It seems counterintuitive, but the more specific your examples are, the easier it is for people to draw broad conclusions.

Marshall Goldsmith's book *What Got You Here Won't Get You There* does a good job of this. He could speak in vagaries about how people need to change, how everyone has a compulsion to share information, and how hard it is for people to see themselves. Instead, he provides specific stories such as sitting at the table with the former CEO of the consultancy McKinsey or the one where a Wall Street hotshot's wife and kids thought he was a jerk at home. Those kinds of where-the-rubber-meets-the-road examples paint a vivid picture of reality.

Stories are the most powerful way to illustrate your points, to communicate your ideas, to win the favor of your reader, and to persuade them to your way of thinking. The best of all are personal examples—things you have experienced first-hand. After even just a couple of years around the topic of your book, you should have collected some stories.

The most effective are specific stories, using your name, the other person's name (or people's names), and being as specific as possible. When I use examples in this book, I talk about "Greg Short" or "Ryan Lowe" so that you can see that these stories are of real people and real situations.

If I do not have permission to explicitly associate myself with an author's book (that's part of the "ghost" in ghostwriter), I will obscure their information to the point where no one could backtrack to discover whom I might be talking about. You may see me referring to a "how to do business in" book or an IT career book. Even though I cannot reveal much about them, being as specific as our agreement and my ethics allow gives you the impression that these are real books.

Plus, the more concrete and detailed a story you provide your reader, the easier it is to recall later. Their recollection will not be one among many vague projects you refer to, but associated with "the Kauffman facilitator" or "the Russian economist."

My author Dr. Karin Stumpf had an example where we added just a few extra details that moved the example from the somewhat abstract to the concrete. In one instance, a sentence from the previous draft read:

I was once hired by a company to provide a workshop to their managers from various levels on how they could coach their own employees.

As generalized as this is, you could imagine any typical corporate scene in any industry with any drab group of executives. To help the reader get a clearer picture, we added a few telling details:

I was once hired by a manufacturing company to provide a workshop in France to engineering managers on how to coach their own employees.

Those three details—a manufacturer, France, and engineers—make this story more real. Instead of a netherworld populated with faceless suits, you see a group of French engineers figuring out how to work better with their production line workers.

Sometimes, you may need to distance yourself from an example but still use it to illustrate your point. It could be that you made a horrible decision that you learned from and want to share, but do not want it to reflect on your reputation. For instance, there have been times I gave a friend advice about a life lesson I learned, but I did not want to share that the person in the story was me. It was too painful or simply too personal. So instead of something happening to me, it happened to "a friend of mine" or "a person I once heard about."

When you do use a story, you do not have to have every detail perfect and transcribe every conversation down to the last "uh." Almost by definition, a story culls the boring and irrelevant, polishing the narrative until it best serves its purpose. When I write about a conversation I had with a client, I cannot remember how the back-and-forth went verbatim. I remember how they spoke and the gist of what they said. Literally recounting the exchange is impossible. So, I may write something along the lines of what our conversation might have looked like to the degree that, if the other person read it, they would say, "Yeah, that's how it happened."

Another storytelling tool is "compression" where the narrator takes a series of events and strings them all together, snipping out the irrelevant middle (a.k.a. "compressing it") so the audience can easily follow the narrative without losing interest.

For instance, one of my clients taught a course spread out over several days. In their book, we recounted a conversation between them and a participant. The exchange was somewhat intimate with the participant dealing with some personal issues. We used this as a true illustration to reach the reader on a deeply emotional level. In reality, though, the conversation did not happen all at once but over the course of the class. We could have tried to retell the story as accurately as possible, but imagine how convoluted that would have been: "On Monday, she said this. On Tuesday morning, she said that, but by Tuesday afternoon she had changed her position to something else. After Wednesday morning breakfast…" By compressing multiple conversations, my author achieved the clarity and intent of the story without substantially altering what happened.

We do this in daily life all the time. When I tell my wife about what a mutual friend of ours said, I do not recount an entire thirty-minute conversation. Instead, I give her the condensed version. When people ask me how I came to live in Baton Rouge, I don't tell them my life story. I hit the highlights of my journey or just say, "Family." I reshape and reorganize the information to be relevant to my listener without obscuring the underlying truth.

MAKE IT ABOUT PEOPLE

Our interest's on the dangerous edge of things,

The honest thief, the tender murderer,

The superstitious atheist.

~ ROBERT BROWNING, "BISHOP BLOUGRAM'S APOLOGY"

Maphead. The book review in *The Seattle Times* said, "It's everything about maps: past, present, and limitless future." So, you might guess that it's about maps.

It's not.

A book about maps would not make me laugh out loud in every chapter. A book about maps would not make me furrow my brow while reading shocking trivia. A book about maps would not bolster my faith in humanity.

No, *Maphead* is not about maps; it's about people who love maps—a subtle but crucial distinction.

The author offered insights into the geocaching community, one million strong, who create global scavenger hunts encompassing all seven continents (yes, that includes Antarctica). He spoke about the minds behind Google Earth and why they are invited to high-level U.N.

diplomatic functions. He walked me through the history of how British postcards won WWII.

After reading so many books filled with facts and statistics, I find it difficult for me to keep figures straight—but I can easily recall the people I read about.

Just a minute ago, I encouraged you to tell stories. You should. And the best stories you can tell are not about corporations, or market shifts, or historical events. The best stories involve people: flesh and blood, living, breathing human beings with hopes, dreams, and ideas.

If you want to write a great book, it needs to be about people. Tell me Justinian wedded Theodora and I yawn. Tell me that a Roman emperor made a stripper his wife and empress of the Byzantine Empire and I am suddenly intrigued. We just went from fact to story.

Patrick Lencioni adroitly takes this idea to a whole new level in business fables. Instead of simply presenting information, he crafts an entire story around the information. My personal favorite is *Getting Naked* that almost reads like Charles Dickens's *The Christmas Carol* in which Ebenezer Scrooge finds redemption and a new life. The story around *Getting Naked*'s hero made me want to finish the book, regardless of what else Lencioni said. Any business book so engrossing that you do not want to put it down is destined to be a success.

It's Your Ship is another fine example. Captain Michael Abrashoff's advice is rooted in the experiences of his interactions with other people under his command. He could have simply presented his management advice, but I would not have connected with the author and his ideas nearly as much. It was his stories about people that made it a wonderful book.

Go ahead and tell us how to implement your proprietary methodology, but make sure you tell us about the people who have done so. Record your company's history, but in addition to listing dates and events, tell us stories about the people who were part of them. Show us how to sell, but relate a story about how you sold to a difficult client.

The father of self-publishing, Dan Poynter, once wrote, "Your reader wants the information; he or she is not reading your nonfiction book to be entertained."

On the surface, that's true. People read business books to solve a problem; they read novels for fun. But as I said earlier, business books have twin goals. The first is to inform; the second is to sell. Your book needs to solve your reader's problem, but it also needs to solve your problem of getting your name out there, earning more respect, and establishing your place in your niche. To do that, people need to connect with more than your information. They need to connect with you. They won't connect with you unless they connect with your book. They won't connect with your book unless they connect with the personal stories in your book.

Or for visual learners:

Reader → *personal stories* → *book* → *author*

Ergo, tell stories about people.

PLAGIARISM AND COPYRIGHT

"Great poets imitate and improve, whereas small ones steal and spoil."
~ W.H. DAVENPORT ADAMS, "IMITATORS AND PLAGIARISTS"

"I've been imitated so well I've heard people copy my mistakes."
~ JIMI HENDRIX

One of my authors substantially changed an entire component in their methodology because the visual looked too much like Jim Collins's Hedgehog Concept.

I did my utmost to convince them that they were needlessly changing their visual and potentially obscuring their ideas. They responded, "Oh, but Derek, I don't want to get into any copyright lawsuits. Better safe than sorry."

Let me put your mind at ease: no one can copyright an idea (nor patent it, for that matter). I discovered that the "taming of the sheafs" process I stumbled across as I tried to make sense of the chaotic mess of a particular manuscript (and then began using for all of the books I worked on) is virtually identical to the "pilot system" espoused by Dan Poynter. Great minds work in the same direction—and because this type of thing happens so often, US legislation does not allow us to patent concepts.

In fact, you cannot even copyright a book title unless you create a series of books under the same title. The *Rich Dad* or *Trump University* books could be copyrighted because they are the titles to a series; *The Fred Factor* and *In Search of Excellence* could not, since those titles were used for just one book.

The main idea behind copyright is that no one else can pass off another author's work as their own. However, copyright law does allow for "fair use," meaning that you may directly quote limited passages from virtually anyone's work without infringing on copyright law.

According to the *Chicago Manual of Style* (16th edition):

> *Essentially, the [fair use] doctrine excuses copying that would otherwise be infringement. For example, it allows authors to quote from other authors' work… for purposes of review or criticism or to illustrate or buttress their own points. Authors invoking fair use should transcribe accurately and give credit to their sources…. As a general rule, one should never quote more than a few continuous paragraphs.*

But here's where it gets murky:

> *Proportion is more important than the absolute length of a quotation; quoting five hundred words from an essay of five thousand is likely to be riskier than quoting that amount from a work of fifty thousand. But an even smaller percentage can be an infringement if it constitutes the heart of the work being quoted.*

In other words, you can quote a paragraph from a John Grisham book without having to pay royalties, ask for permission, or breaking any kind of law—but only because the book is novel length.

Contrast that against quoting Ashleigh Brilliant's "brilliant thoughts in seventeen words or less," such as this gem: "More books have resulted from somebody's need to write than from anybody's need to read." While one of his books may have hundreds of such quotes, each of them constitutes the heart of his work. If everyone could quote all of them, he would never be recompensed for sharing his ideas with the world. As such, you cannot reprint Ashleigh's Brilliant Thoughts without infringing on his copyright.[8]

Songs, however, have their own unique set of rules. In the US and the UK, at least, song titles are not protected by law. If you want to name each of your chapters with a song title, go ahead. The lyrics of the song, though, are protected.

For example, I can tell you that my daughter and I sing the chorus of "Hotel California" together, but I can't tell you what the words of that chorus are. I can allude to the fact that it starts by welcoming you to the establishment, and remarking on a lovely place and face, with plenty of vacancies available throughout the year able to be found there...but that's as far as intellectual property laws allow me to go.

Speaking of workarounds, allow me to point out that copyright laws apply to directly quoting someone else's material. Those laws have nothing to do with the ideas behind their words (as I just demonstrated). Legally[9], their ideas are fair game. My author could have copied Jim Collins's Hedgehog Concept, changed the words around, and presented it as her own.

---

[8] Yes, I paid Ashleigh for the right to use his quote.

[9] In case you missed the disclaimer: I am not a lawyer. My legal education consists of one business law class taught by Steve Hearn, the assistant district attorney for Lincoln Parish. Incidentally, he was one of the most interesting teachers I've ever had.

Ethically, though, I would never encourage nor condone an author outright stealing someone else's ideas. However, as we discussed earlier, it is perfectly fine to adapt or build on their ideas, stories, or examples to support, illustrate, or buttress your own ideas.

So relax. Credit your sources, but don't live in constant fear of being sued by another writer.

EASTER EGGS VS. IRRELEVANT REFERENCES

> *"Dissecting humor is like dissecting a frog.*
> *No one enjoys it and the frog dies."*
> ~ ATTRIBUTED TO E.B. WHITE

Few things irritate me as much as an author trying to make a joke but having to explain it because it refers to such an obscure jingle, song, or TV commercial.

If you want to quote, do it; no need to credit the artist, the songwriter, the producer, and the makeup lady. "I once heard a great line from a movie" is really all anyone needs to know. You do not have to actually name the movie. And definitely don't something as awful as: "Okay, we're about to dive into my leadership process. But are you ready? Like Leonardo DiCaprio's character said in James Cameron's 1997 blockbuster hit *Titanic*: I need you to hold on!"

See how unwieldy and misdirecting that is?

If you feel that you must reference something, do it as concisely as possible. Something as simple as, "Like they said in *Titanic*: I need you to hold on!" will suffice.

If it takes you forever to tell a joke, make a quip, or reference a humorous line, it takes all the fun out.

On the other hand, I do enjoy finding "Easter eggs." In videogames, an Easter egg is a hidden joke or an "extra" available to players if they go through a certain series of actions. These are usually jokes or special messages from game designers to the players. In an early Atari game, for example, a certain pixel would take you to a secret room with the words "Created by Warren Robinett," one of the original developers.

Books often have these, too. In *The Courtship of Princess Leia*, set after the events of the original *Star Wars* trilogy, Han Solo goes by the alias Jenos Idanian—an anagram of Indiana Jones, the other character we remember Harrison Ford for.

Movies abound with Easter eggs. Alfred Hitchcock was famous for his cameo appearances in his own movies. *Rocky Horror*, *Fight Club*, and nearly every modern Disney and Pixar movie have some hidden inside jokes scattered throughout the scenes.

I'm not suggesting you create something elaborate. My Easter eggs are hidden in plain sight, so unobtrusive that most people would not give them a second thought, but plain enough for people "in the know." I might casually mention "the sugar to help the medicine go down," a line from *Mary Poppins*, a movie that evokes some great childhood memories for me.[10] But I do not go through the whole spiel.

In *The Future of Management*, Gary Hamel penned the line, "It's not filled with exhortations to 'go thou and do likewise.'" This phrase comes from the King James version of the gospel of Luke, but Gary didn't stop to explain that. Even if you didn't understand the reference, you still understood what he said.

If someone gets it, great; if not, then it does not trip them up as they continue to read.

SAY IT LOUD!

> *"If you don't know how to pronounce a word, say it loud! If you don't know how to pronounce a word, say it loud!"*
> ~ WILLIAM STRUNK, *THE ELEMENTS OF STYLE*

---

[10]Notice that it is an allusion, not an exact quote. Keep those intellectual property rights in mind.

Can't you imagine a 1960s classroom with a professor in horn-rimmed glasses, hands flat on his desk, yelling at his students, "Say it loud!"

Professor Strunk "felt it was worse to be irresolute than to be wrong," which is quite different from what I was taught as a graduate student. Academia forces you to write in an indefinite tone. Because they focus on the pursuit of knowledge, a scholar can never be sure about anything. Nothing simply is; it "may be," or it "has been said." You do not definitively know; you "suggest," you "posit," you "hypothesize." Some things are even "near certain," but absolutely nothing is absolute.

I understand the underlying reason: you never want to be sure of anything because as soon as you feel something is "for certain," you preclude discovering anything new. Hedging everything you think or observe in indefinite terms keeps you on your toes.

That's the theory, at least.

I could write an entire chapter on why that practice is more harmful than helpful and why it doesn't accomplish its purpose, even in the ivory tower. Let me simply say this: if you're writing a business book, be definite, even when you write to an academic audience. Write with authority. Write with confidence.

Anthropologists can afford to be uncertain; business authors cannot.

Confidence can make up for a lot of failings. Something about it inexorably attracts us. It's why we instinctively distrust mealy-mouthed people scared of their own shadow. It's why we depict our leaders with their shoulders squared, chin jutted out in defiance, in a Superman stance, ready to take on the world. We want the people we follow to be sure of themselves, their purpose, and their destination.

I know it is scary to make a statement with little concrete evidence to back it. With nearly every sentence I write, an imaginary critic punches holes in it, picks it apart, and leaves it on the ground, gasping for its breath. I hear imaginary people arguing it from sixteen different angles.

But I am not writing to silence my critics (real or imaginary). I do not write to convince my adversaries (almost all of which are imaginary). I write for my reader.

As such, I am vigilant to strike phrases like the following from my work and from my clients':

- "Don't take my word for it…"

- "I am convinced…"

- "I believe…" (or, even better: "I *firmly* believe…")

- "I could be wrong…"

- "I feel…"

- "I suggest…"

- "I think…"

- "In my opinion…"

- "It may be…"

- "My belief is that…"

With few exceptions, the entire book you hold in your hands is my opinion. Now, my opinion is based on extensive professional experience and observation gathered from my time working with business authors and learning from some of the most skilled people in the publishing industry. It is an amalgamation of everything I have seen, heard, read, said, done, and lived. Technically, though, little of it can be attributed to verifiable, scientifically reproducible facts.

Do I really have to preface every sentence with, "In my opinion…"? It's my name on the cover: of course it's my opinion. Who else's would it be?

No one is omniscient. Therefore, you can safely assume that when you state something that is not a verifiable, scientific fact, you say it with the implicit understanding that you are not God. The business trade audience is mature enough that you do not have to treat them as if they were eighth graders reading your book as the gospel. You could be wrong. You could be so far out in left field that you're not even in the ballpark—

...but there is no reason to constantly call attention to that fact.

Don't write your book for your critics. Write your book for people who need, want, and welcome your words.

SOUND BITE SUMMARY

- ✦ Write the first draft for yourself. Rewrite it for your reader.

- ✦ When you write a book, set the hook.

- ✦ You don't need to spend chapter one defining the problem—your reader is neck-deep in it already.

- ✦ Trust your instincts.

- ✦ Don't worry about people stealing your ideas. Focus on delivering incredible insights.

- ✦ Don't write out of fear.

- ✦ People can't connect with information. They connect only with stories.

- ✦ Your reader will learn faster from a specific example than an abstract principle.

- ✦ Reshape and reorganize stories to be relevant to your reader without obscuring the underlying truth.

- ✦ Make your book not about facts and information but about people and life.

- ✦ Write with authority.

- ✦ Don't write your book for your critics. Write your book for people who need, want, and welcome your words.

7

HOW DO I FIGHT WRITER'S BLOCK AND KEEP WRITING?

"I write only when inspiration strikes. Fortunately it strikes every morning at nine o'clock sharp."

~ ATTRIBUTED TO WILLIAM FAULKNER[1]

OW IN THE WORLD did I gain a hundred pounds? Admittedly, I was bound to gain a few pounds after high school, but still—that's an unhealthy amount of extra weight.

But who has the time to be healthy? I have a wife to charm, two kids to chase, a mortgage to pay, a yard to keep, a church to support, family to visit, a business to run, school functions to attend, friendships to maintain, books to read, authors to help…where in the midst of all that would I find the time to exercise?

---

[1] And often incorrectly to W. Somerset Maugham

Without exercise, though, I continued to be overweight, to have trouble sleeping, to stay tense, to avoid the mirror as much as possible, and to generally stay exhausted.

Not that smart, is it?

The truth is that I started getting healthy when I decided to get healthy. One day, I decided to return to martial arts. Amazingly, I still got everything accomplished that I did before. I didn't have to neglect my children. I didn't see a decline in business. I didn't steal time away from the important things. In fact, just about every area of my life saw improvement. I had more energy, more confidence, and more focus.

Where did that time come from? I don't know, but I'm glad it showed up.

Writing is quite the same way. "Finding the time" is the most common challenge would-be authors voice. Make no mistake: it is time-consuming.

But when I am excited about a new idea for a book or new project of my own, I suddenly seem to find the time. Getting up early is easy, even if I went to bed too late the night before. Finding five or ten minutes to write in my binder is suddenly not so hard. I get in a few minutes while waiting at my daughter's gymnastics class or in the car while Amanda runs into the store. The more excited I am, the easier it seems to be to find those spare moments. Like spare change, it can quickly add up to serious dough. And doing so hasn't diminished anything else in my life or business.

If you cannot seem to find the time, the real culprit is that you cannot find the motivation. If you're not excited about your book, you need to find the real reason. I suggest reading *The Artist's Way* by Julia Cameron. The book you want to write already exists in your subconscious. Your job is to dig it out of there and get it onto paper. If you have writer's block, the problem is not that you don't know what to write, but that you cannot get past your mental block to dig down into your subconscious to pull it out.

I ghostwrite for my client-authors every day. Every single day of the week, I have to translate their thoughts, words, stories, explanations, etc. into a deliverable to keep them happy. It's not magic. It's work.

But to really understand what's going on with your writer's block, I need to introduce you to two people: the Critic and the Muse.

The Critique of the Critic, the Musing of the Muse

"This is the other secret that real artists know and wannabe writers don't. When we sit down each day and do our work, power concentrates around us. The Muse takes note of our dedication. She approves. We have earned favor in her sight. When we sit down and work, we become like a magnetized rod that attracts iron filings. Ideas come."
~ Steven Pressfield, *The War of Art*

You've watched cartoons where the hero faced a moral dilemma and a little angel suddenly appears on one shoulder and a little devil appears on the other. The angel urges the hero to do the right thing while the devil appeals to their bad side. (Usually, the devil wins out.)

As you write, you will encounter two such ethereal beings with pretty similar personalities. My friend, allow me to introduce the Critic and the Muse.

You have them, whether you acknowledge their presence or not. The Critic is that loud voice in your ear, making you second-guess every word you write, every thought you have, and every decision you make. The Muse whispers in your other ear, encouraging and inspiring you to do great things and write wonderful words.

They have a symbiotic relationship with you, but it is up to you to make sure that relationship stays in harmony. The Critic is aggressive; the Muse, shy. The more you allow the Critic to speak, the less often the Muse speaks. If all she ever hears is how stupid she is, she eventually learns to stay silent. The Critic cowers her into submission.

Then again, if you always put your hands over your ears and sing "La-la-la" to drown out the Critic's critiques, then you will never refine your writing into something truly great. It will look great to you and your Muse (as everyone's own writing does—nobody ever believes they have an ugly baby), but it will look immature and unpolished to the rest of the world.

As much as we hate the Critic and as flighty as the Muse is, we need them both—just not at the same time. While the Critic is an invaluable ally, he must remain silent while my Muse is pontificating. The Critic gets to speak at the appropriate time, days, weeks, or even months later. Not before.

Maybe your Muse is a cigar-smoking, basement-dwelling man, like Stephen King's. Maybe your Critic is a woman, like those old-school Catholic school marms. Julia Cameron calls hers the Censor. Maybe the Muse and the Critic are the schizophrenic sides of your old Aunt Hilda. Maybe you've never sat down to really get to know either one.

However you envision them, use them to make your writing great. Let your Muse inspire great thoughts, and then let your Critic refine them into great writing. Together, they can help you overcome writer's block, stay motivated, and overcome the other challenges you will encounter as you write.

THE TRUTH ABOUT WRITER'S BLOCK AND BAD WRITING

"Fear is at the root of most bad writing."
~ STEPHEN KING, *ON WRITING*

Writer's block is the manifestation of our own fears. When we are afraid, the Critic quickly takes a seat beside us, whispering that we have nothing to say or that the book is taking forever. He paralyzes us with even more fear.

When I write, the Critic always stands behind me, peering over my shoulder. While I am giving a piece of advice, he might say, "Yeah, you're saying that, but we could argue the point. In fact, don't even make an original point—it leaves you too wide open for attack. Instead, let's go find someone else who's written something and tear them apart."

Anyone can argue. Entire books have been written as counterarguments to someone else's thoughts (think talk show hosts). I've been tempted to write sections of this book arguing against other people's points. For example, I once read an article by an author I respect who advised his followers that not only should they write a book, they should write it from start to finish in a matter of weeks. While his reasons have merit, I believe in a more reasoned approach.

It is tempting to argue as a stand-in for original thinking. For one, it gives you something to speak to. Instead of creating your own material, all you have to do is argue the other side. You do not have to be creative; the other guy (or gal) has already laid out the structure you need to follow. You could spend pages taking their article apart and presenting a counterpoint to each of their reasons. You could easily write an entire chapter as a one-sided debate.

When you feel yourself arguing on paper, remember two things:

1. That other guy or gal is not your reader.
2. Arguing is easy; original thought is not.

Arguing comes from a need to write defensively.

The need to write defensively really comes from writing out of fear. Fear that our peers will rip our ideas to shreds. Fear that our mentors will laugh at our clumsy attempt to express ourselves. Fear that we will stand in front of the world like the embarrassed royal in "The Emperor's New Clothes," hoping against hope that no one will realize how unprepared, vulnerable, and naked we really are.

So instead of sharing our own ideas, we ridicule others'. Instead of taking a stand on an issue, we give ourselves enough latitude to quickly retreat from a stance if it becomes untenable. In place of a manuscript that confidently presents and advances a new idea, we wind up with a diluted book that does nothing, says nothing, establishes nothing—but hey, at least no one can say anything bad about it, right?

You're not writing for your critics.

A simple statement, yet these six words summarize a swath of this book.

I once worked with an author who constantly referred to the people who would criticize his book when it came out. It seemed like a big motivator for him was to shut his critics up. Often, his criterion for deciding to include something was how it would be perceived by this imaginary crowd in his head. Would they be able to twist it into something insidious? Would they tear it apart and expose him as a fraud? Would they remember an incident slightly differently and call him out?

As an author, you simply cannot allow fear to guide the crafting of your book.

I understand being sensitive to potential critics, known and unknown. I once worked with an executive whose book would potentially be read by the leaders of one of the world's largest economies and gain national attention, especially in business circles. We were particularly aware of how many might take exception to any number of points he made. We smoothed over the rough edges and—to my constant annoyance—necessarily modified many assertions.

Finally, I said, "Luke, you're not writing this book for the people who are going to hate it anyway. You're writing it for your readers, for the companies and leaders and people who need to know all of this, regardless of how ugly or politically incorrect any of it may be. If you write a book that everyone loves, you'll wind up with a travel brochure that says, 'This country is lovely. Come visit.' And little else." To my gratification, he did not back down from some rather bold statements. His book was richer for them.

Believe it or not, not being able to say anything good about your book is worse than not being able to say anything at all. If you elicit some controversy, you will elicit some attention. (Hey, some people might even buy your book just so they can weigh in on the feeding frenzy, too. This is the kind of thinking behind the adage "There is no such thing as bad publicity.")

Here is an obvious truth: we write out of fear because we are afraid. But what are we afraid of? Disapproval? Disagreement? Disdain?

If your book is any good, it will inevitably attract attention. Statistically, someone out there will criticize you. But you did not write your book for them. They do not matter. Do not argue with people, fictitious or real. Do not picture a mob tearing your book apart before storming your home with torches and pitchforks.

Your book is supposed to help your reader—the person drowning and desperately in need of a lifeline. Picture someone sitting at a coffee shop, intently reading your book, and coming across a sentence that turns the light bulb on over their head and puts a smile on their face. That is your reader—the person who needs, wants, and welcomes your words.

If fear is at the root of bad writing, then confidence is at the root of good writing. Or, in other words, confidence is the basis of creativity.

WRITING BY NOT WRITING

"Writers often say, truthfully, that they are as much at work away from their desks as in the act of writing itself."

~ PAUL HORGAN

There is an eclectic collection of shops near downtown Baton Rouge called Circa 1857. They comprise most of a city block and include an architectural salvage business, multiple art galleries, niche antique dealers, a café, a frame shop, and the booths of local artisans and merchants. The place is downright funky. I always feel a bit more human after leaving.

Believe me, I find it strange that a trip to look at brass knobs, watercolors, and a Tin Man made out of tin cans helps me ghostwrite about data analytics or economics—but it does.

You'll find that battling writer's block doesn't always look the same for you. Sometimes one tactic will work for a while, and then sometimes it takes something completely new.

As I shared earlier, I don't begin a book by writing the first word of chapter one. Rather, I write plenty of things related to the book that may never reach the final draft. I simply write stream-of-consciousness. I usually start with a particular topic, but I often meander into a sidebar discussion. This way, I short-circuit my writer's block. By not forcing myself to write finished prose, there's no pressure to trigger that paralyzing feeling.

Later, I'll split the two discussions up: in that moment, I let my subconscious get its ideas out. It comes sporadically, but no matter. I'd rather be setting it all out in a jumble than staring at the blank page, waiting for the perfect word. I shared this quote by Goran "George" Moberg earlier, but it bears repeating: "Don't get it right. Get it written, then get it right."

Julia Cameron taught me to do the Morning Pages wherein you write/journal every morning. I think she specifies three pages. I also think she means three journal-sized pages. Dummy me, when I began, all I had at hand was a legal pad, so I forced myself to write three legal-sized pages every morning. It took forever but it was a wonderful lesson in how *not* stopping eventually produced something good. Sometimes what I wrote was mere drivel or, literally, "I don't know what else to write. I think I've said all I can think of to say." But that one statement would remind me of the line "There's nothing more I can think of to say to you" from *Don't Cry for Me Argentina*. That would, in turn, spur some other thoughts.

In other words, when I gave myself no other choice but to write, I wrote.

When I hit some writer's block in the middle of my book, I fall back on this strategy. I take out a sheet of paper and write in stream-of-consciousness. If something about my book comes out of it, great.

Regardless, just to have my gears spinning and my pen moving helps get the creative juices flowing again and gives the Muse some space to ramble.

You should practice the above in longhand, but when that peters out, switch to the keyboard and type yourself to exhaustion. Again, the quality does not matter so much as the quantity. By throwing everything possible onto the table, you will surely have a gem in there when you come back to sort through it all.

My second method of fighting the block is to sleep on it. From the original self-help book *The New Psycho-Cybernetics*, I learned to trust my subconscious. The authors helped me get into the habit of writing down what I wanted to write and ghostwrite about the next day. Not in excruciating detail—just enough to know what I meant. The next day when I sit at the keyboard, the words sometimes tumble out of me. It works.

Third, I walk away.

I've read about musicians taking time off to "replenish the creative well." *What a load of crock*, I used to think. *Singing and writing songs all day—yeah, what a hard life.*

They were right. From time to time, we draw too much from the creative wellspring of our Muse and need to refill the source. Taking time away from a creative endeavor helps, but it is better to actively fill the well by doing something that feeds your soul. Find a funky art co-op. Have a game night with your family. Read a book just for fun. Go engage in a hobby or sport you enjoy. Cook a new dish. Call up an old friend. Pull up a chair and watch the sunset.

Do what works for you.

Find a Reason to Write

"I don't read business books. And I almost never talk to anyone who reads them."

~ Nassim Nicholas Taleb, author of *The Black Swan*

"I usually tell people not to read business books at all. They're just ego trips. You're not going to learn anything."
~ BOB MACDONALD, AUTHOR OF *CHEAT TO WIN*

These two quotes opened a *BusinessWeek* article on how to write a business bestseller. It provided such gems as "animal metaphors are still the industry standard" and "buy your own books." I read the rest of the article, knowing it had to be a joke.

If it was, the writer forgot the punch line.

I agree that many business books published should never have seen the light of day. They are, indeed, ego trips. Some were written just so they could say they were an author. In fact, I'm sure some have released plenty of such books, knowing, or perhaps even hoping, that no one would read them.

Let me draw your attention to the fact that this is true across all genres. I cannot imagine how romance writers come up with new plots. You would think that after a few thousand romance novels, the Department of Fresh Ideas would be fresh out. Yet romance continues to compose about half—yes, half!—of the fiction market. On the other side of the bookstore, self-help relationship books dominate much of nonfiction sales. How many ways can you help people fall in love and stay there?

There are great romance books (yes, I admit to reading one or two) and some much-needed advice in select relationship books (I have to read these to keep finding new ways to charm my wife). But for every good one, there are at least ten dozen that should be burned so that future generations won't find them and say, "Our ancestors spent their time and money to read this stuff?"

You could say the same for all fields of human endeavor. Music, art, architecture, landscaping, sculpting, legislation, and design—much of it lies on the scale somewhere between awful and ordinary. If you were Tchaikovsky and took Taleb's advice, you would never listen to any other musicians—ever. If you were Monet and took MacDonald's advice, you would never look at anyone else's art. After all, aren't all songs and paintings just ego trips for the artist?

Blanket statements like theirs reveal the speaker's cynicism. It's like saying all New Yorkers are heartless or all farmers are country hicks. Such sweeping generalizations are ludicrous.

Many business books have left me unchanged, like a certain internet marketing book I have in mind as I write this. But plenty of them deeply inspired me. They gave me permission to be an entrepreneur, to aspire to more, and to find my own path instead of following the one laid out for me by society. Reading about business owners who bucked the way things were done and experienced profound success provides a clue that there is more than one road to achievement.

You must find meaning in your work. You have to believe in something. You have to know that what you're doing serves a purpose—that to whatever degree, it somehow makes the world a better place.

No doubt many would find it laughable that I find deep meaning in writing and ghostwriting business books. I mean, it's not like I fight fires or save children or rescue the homeless. You can't place what I do in that "everyday hero" category. I'm just a guy with a pen.

But to understand why I feel like what I do matters, think about Super Bowl ads. As of this writing, they cost about $3 million per thirty-second spot. While there have been some clear winners, nearly everyone can name an ad that flopped. In fact, there are multiple top ten fail lists on the internet that never overlap with each other.

Ostensibly, the purpose of a Super Bowl ad is to boost a company's sales, or at least to boost their brand recognition such that it leads to a massive boost in sales. Those ads are a type of investment that are supposed to enjoy a return. But when an ad flops and fails, the company has, at best, wasted $3 million; at worst, it might have sounded its death knell.

That $3 million was supposed to earn the company more money. More money means more opportunities for more people. When the manufacturer my father works for expanded, he was part of the team that built a new plant in Thailand. My family lived there only for a short while, but it was the first time I had traveled outside of the US. That international experience changed the course of my life.

An expanding business means more job security for the people there. I have been part of a crumbling company before and it's not pretty.

A successful company means more entry-level positions or part-time positions. As a student and college graduate, I have looked for both and wished I could have found more.

More money means the ability to do innovative things, to take risks a company otherwise could not afford to. As a self-employed professional with roller coaster revenue, I like when I have the option to do cool stuff that might seriously propel my business forward instead of having to just foot the bills and play it safe.

But when your company wastes $3 million on an ad that never brings in additional revenue, then those millions of dollars have to come out of bonus checks, expansion plans, training, and everywhere else.

I have never ghostwritten a book on how to design an effective Super Bowl ad…but I have helped plenty of authors show business owners and professionals how to not waste millions of dollars and how to more effectively use the resources they have to make millions more.

I do not delude myself into imagining I am some sort of economic superhero. I highly doubt that a company will be completely revolutionized by one executive reading just one book. Even a business book that sold a million copies would only reach 0.017 percent of the global population. But I do believe my authors' books lead to better business practices that, in turn, lead to creating more value to the people influenced by those businesses.

I'm not trying to change the whole world—just a few people in it. I believe that my clients' books help their respective reader make better business decisions. That, in turn, leads to a more prosperous business. The more prosperity there is in the world, the more lives can be improved by it.

That's what I do with my life…and when I think about the big picture, I'm inspired to write a little more.

SOUND BITE SUMMARY

- ◆ You'll never have time to write.

- ◆ Writing is not art—it's work.

- ◆ You need the musings of the Muse and the critique of the Critic. It's up to you to keep them in harmony.

- ◆ Confidence is the basis of creativity.

- ◆ Don't write defensively.

- ◆ There are ways around writer's block. Find the one that works for you.

- ◆ Find your reason to write.

8

HOW DO I MAKE IT SOUND GREAT?

"Have something to say, and say it as clearly as you can. That is the only secret to style."
~ MATTHEW ARNOLD, *COLLECTIONS AND RECOLLECTIONS*

"It is the writer's fault, not the reader's, if the reader puts down the book."
~ DAVID HALBERSTAM

WHEN MY MOTHER WAS A LITTLE GIRL, her family lived not too far from the train tracks. Sometimes her brothers would place pennies on the rails for the trains to roll over. Urban legend has it that a coin on the tracks will derail the entire train, sending it hurtling through the air like a scene straight out of an action thriller. The truth is that the train just flattens the pennies, cutting two arrow-straight lines through the middle. I have quite a few as a testament to the fact.[1]

---

[1] If anyone from the Federal Railroad Administration happens to read this, the statute of limitations on my mother and her family ran out long ago, so don't even think about it.

Small change on the tracks can't derail a train, but small things on the page can derail a train of thought.

You want your reader to achieve "flow." That's what I call it when I glide effortlessly through a book. The words are so spot on, the sentences so rhythmic, the punctuation so perfect, that I forget I'm even reading. I am so in-sync with the author that it feels like I'm watching a movie.

But a mangled thought, a clumsily bridged gap, or a badly worded sentiment brings me crashing back to reality.

A reader should never have to stop to figure out what you mean. Edit until your writing is so smooth they forget they're even reading. Everything that makes that journey "unsmooth" distracts them. Typos, for instance, put little red flags in your reader's mind. It makes them wonder how professional the manuscript is. Line editing is important, too. The more clear, concise, and powerful your statements are, the better.

But these levels of editing are further down the line. Before you can even begin to worry about word choice—before you can get to "finish work," as I put it—you need to address the structural issues, content gaps, flow of ideas, and overall tone of your work.

Writing out of fear, inserting needless opinions, misdirecting the focus of a story, restating the same point—all of these things must be fixed before you can even begin to worry about whether to use "compose" or "comprise" in a sentence.

There are two parts to every book: what you say and how you say it. In chapter six, we talked about what to say. To write a great business book, you must first have something valuable to impart. After you figure out what to say, then you can worry about how to say it. That's what editing is about.

Make it easy for them to stay with you until the very end.

TRANSITIONS

"Look on every exit as being an entrance somewhere else."
~ TOM STOPPARD, *ROSENCRANTZ AND GUILDENSTERN ARE DEAD*

How do I turn my Frankendrafts into highly polished manuscripts?

I have a confession to make: I use a bit of sleight of hand to make my books and my clients' books work. There is so much information, so many ideas, and so many stories to share that it gets pretty challenging to present all of it in an orderly, sequential flow where one example perfectly sets up the following section that neatly segues into the next.

I do my best, but again, writing a business book is more like bringing life to Frankenstein than painting the Mona Lisa.

If you could see some of my Frankendrafts, you would shudder at how raw they look. Before I send the first chapter draft to a new client, I have a little spiel I go through about how the final product may look nothing like what they are about to see. The first draft is "throwing paint on the canvas"—just something tangible to have a conversation around.

But if you were to create an outline summary of my Frankendraft and compare it to an outline summary of the finished version, you would be amazed at how closely they resemble each other. The ideas are often in the same order. Conceptually, the rough version and the finished version are close siblings, if not twins.

But on paper, the two are light years apart. One is an assortment of scattered thoughts; the other, a polished presentation of brilliance. Before the editing, the book flowed logically, but it seemed abrupt. One moment you might be reading about the Dark Ages and the next, baseball. Both sections were where they needed to be, but there was nothing bridging the two.

Suddenly switching from one line of thought to another is like forcing your reader to jump from one speeding train to another. While they may make the leap, they will be disoriented for a moment. Do this often enough, and your reader will finally disembark for good.

The secret is in the transitions. You can make any two pieces of writing work together—if you know how to bridge the gap (or jump the tracks).

When you are having a conversation with someone and they abruptly begin talking about a completely different subject, you are momentarily lost as you try to understand the relevance of the new conversation to the previous one. We are disoriented without some kind of preface like, "Oh, that reminds me...", "Speaking of, did you know...", or at least, "I don't know why that made me think of this, but..." By giving us at least a hint that the conversation is changing direction, it does not feel like such a leap to go from one idea to another.

Provide the same courtesy to your reader. If you make an analogy, spell it out: "Just as a lack of literacy stifled innovation in the Dark Ages, a lack of information sharing has stifled innovation in baseball." It may be a tenuous bridge, but it's a bridge nonetheless.

Every sentence, paragraph, and chapter needs to either set up your reader for the next one, take its cue from the previous one, or at least give them some sign to let them reorient themselves.

You could rewrite whole swaths of copy to ease the transition, but I find that a simple one- or two-sentence bridge will often do the trick. If I can easily and simply state the logical shift from this idea to that one, why complicate it? Something as simple as this would work: "Now that I have discussed the geology of oil shale, let me present the economics of..."

Of course, not every transition needs a specific signal that you are moving from one thought to another. Some ideas naturally lead into the next. If you can do it smoothly and subtly, so much the better.

If you cannot find a way to make a decent transition, you may need a subhead. Subheads allow you to make a clean break between sections of writing and explicitly advertise: "Now Entering New Territory."

Like so...

Endings

"Usually, when people get to the end of a chapter, they close the book and go to sleep. I deliberately write a book so when the reader gets to the end of the chapter, he or she must turn one more page."

~ Sidney Sheldon

My old business partner taught me two important things about working with people. First, when you meet someone that you may do business with, do some digging around on the internet to find out as much about them as possible—especially potential clients. I never cease to be amazed by how much is out there.

For instance, one time I received an email from a gentleman about a cognitive science book he had in mind. After following a trail across four different websites, I finally found out who he was: the founder of a very well-known software company. Not the size of Microsoft or anything like that, but big enough that most business professionals would recognize the name. Knowing that, I was in a much better position to understand where he was coming from and what the best approach would be for exploring how to work together.

Second, my business partner taught me to wait for the other person to hang up first. Apparently, I had the bad habit of hanging up too quickly. If I thought the conversation was over, I said, "Okay," and *CLICK!*, that was it. When I took an unscientific poll of my friends and family, they agreed with him. I always hung up too abruptly, making them feel as if I were "hanging up" on them.

(Which, I would argue, is the whole point of hanging up…but I digress.)

I took his advice and now wait until the other person hangs up before ending the call. This sometimes makes for rather lengthy and awkward goodbyes, but at least everyone gets off the phone feeling good, instead of thinking what a rude little snot I am.

But I truly did not understand what my friends were saying until I began ghostwriting the end of book chapters. Ending a chapter without any kind of wrap-up feels much the same way my friends felt about the end of our calls: abrupt, unfinished, and mildly disorienting.

An ending to a chapter is like a period on sentence: it signals "Stop Here."

Your endings could be something elaborate, like asking a question throughout the chapter and finally answering it, or weaving a story in and out until it comes to its conclusion. It could be something straight-forward, like a recap of the chapter.[2]

STRIDE BOLDLY AND APOLOGIZE TO NO ONE

"That's the secret to performance: conviction.
The right note played tentatively still misses its mark,
but play boldly and no one will question you."
~ RACHEL HARTMAN, *SERAPHINA*

Do not apologize for your book.

Some authors put what amounts to a disclaimer at the beginning of their book calling attention to everything it lacks. Some authors say that their manuscript is "necessarily broad" because there is not enough time or space to sufficiently delve into every aspect of social media marketing / organizational leadership / small business finance / public speaking / whatever. They say no one book could cover the entire subject.

Well, duh.

Do you think someone will get to the end of your book and say, "Well, I thought it was really too broad and it didn't give me enough specific advice…but they set my expectations low from the outset, so I guess that makes it alright."

Do not apologize for your book. If your reader is not mature and experienced enough to know that your book is not the world's treatise on the subject, then you need to find another audience.

But the issue is really not your reader. When you are tempted to do something along these lines, the true problem is that you are fearful of what you think your reader will think. You are afraid people will criticize your book for what it lacks. You imagine some of them sitting around the table, laughing about how shallow your material or advice is.

Forget them.

---

[2] See? Did you feel like I had set you up for more but left you hanging? Even chapter sections need some kind of wrap-up or transition. Otherwise, it feels like the author forgot to finish.

When you write a business book, people expect to read from the authority on the subject. Whether it be your company's history, a concept you're advancing, research you're presenting, or advice you're offering, people want to know they're reading an expert opinion.

Many authors make timid assertions. They make a statement, preceded or followed by a disclaimer that essentially says they could be wrong. Of course they could be wrong. Everyone could be wrong about everything. All of reality could be a dream à la *The Matrix*.

Don't weaken your influence by apologizing upfront or inserting disclaimer after disclaimer. By justifying everything, you only show that you're not confident in your opinion, even if you really are.

In the section on "Say It Loud!" I listed some phrases that weaken your stance. Here are some more I edited out of a client's manuscript:

+ "For the most part, they are all largely still focused on providing..."

+ "Because of my personal experiences in this area, I firmly believe that..."

+ "The vast majority of _____ can generally be improved."

When you do this it seems as if you're constantly apologizing for not relating absolute truths upon which someone could stake their lives. No one can guarantee that. Why qualify every statement?

Let's rewrite those statements with confidence:

From	To
For the most part, they are all largely still focused on providing...	*They still focus on...*
Because of my personal experiences in this area, I firmly believe that...	*Nothing: cut it entirely and start with the rest of the sentence from that point*
The vast majority of _____ can generally be improved.	*_____ can be improved.*

In a speech or on a phone call, it's okay to temper your position or to preface your words with a disclaimer. It's a different medium and people will receive it differently. But in an authoritative book, your reader wants authoritative advice—not some mewling amateur hoping someone will believe them.

GO FOR GRACIOUS

> *"When asked after a lecture if he meant to imply that a hated academic rival was always wrong, Faraday glowered at the questioner and replied, 'He's not that consistent.'"*
> ~ ROBERT CIALDINI, *INFLUENCE*

One of my all-time favorite novels is *Shōgun*, set in Japan in the 1600s. Besides the intricate plot, enthralling story lines, and the undergirding love story, I love the civility of the language. The Japanese depicted by the author were polite to an extreme. Even when they were getting ready to chop off someone's head, the dialogue went something like, "I'm so sorry, Keiko-san, but I must decapitate you now. Please move your hair away from your neck. So sorry." If two samurai were about to duel to the death, they were civil—courteous, even.

Or, as I like to think of it: gracious.

Being gracious comes from a state of mind. For the purpose of our discussion here, it is a blend of professionalism and the social graces. As the scenes of *Shōgun* beautifully demonstrate, the art of being gracious overlaps with the idea of "face" in Asia.

Face is the amount of respect you have and the measure of your stature in your community (however you define it). When you lose your temper and make a scene, you lose face; when you respectfully finish a negotiation with both sides' reputations intact, you gain face. It is a combination of courtesy, respect, esteem, and competence.

Of course, we have similar social rules in the West. I like the story a sociology professor once told my class about two professors. One had observed a tribe of island natives. In his published journal paper, among other observations, he noted that "the feet of the natives are large."

The other professor challenged his paper with the point of view that his observations were subjective. He could have stopped his response at the logical and excellent argument that social scientists should be as objective as possible. Admittedly, it is a good point, and he could have made it professionally.

But he took it a step further: he went so far as to title his satirical critique as "The Feet of the Natives Are Large." His title was derisive, the academic equivalent of "you moron."

Why did he feel the need to take it from academic response to stinging retort? Why did he get personal? Why was he so…ungracious?

Yes, the original professor was publicly embarrassed at the faux pas. But were I in his academic circles, I would have lost respect for the critic. By shaming his peer, he himself lost face.

You can respectfully disagree with another author without resorting to personal epithets. You can gently debunk someone else's work in a way that allows both parties to save face.

When you write your book, be kind. Be charitable. Don't publish something written out of anger or hate. Publish something that will reflect well on you when your grandchildren read it decades from now.

Sometimes, the situation does call for the direct approach. You may have to disagree with a colleague's findings or need to set the record straight. You can still be gracious even while disagreeing. If you are going to disagree with someone, then argue with their points, not with them personally.

Do not make it emotional. If you disagree with their facts, then present just the facts, ma'am. If you disagree with their opinion, then calmly lay out your perspective. If your experience is at odds with theirs, then it is up to your audience to decide whom to believe.

Being gracious means being courteous even when the other person is being a jerk. It means not allowing your civility to be determined by whoever is in front of you. It means setting the comfort of those around you ahead of your need to put someone in their place. Being gracious means staying composed regardless of the situation. It means never saying, "I told you so."

Graciousness means not being the jerk you want to be.

It is not about being a pushover or an easy mark. It is not about pleasing others and catering to others' whims. In fact, being gracious takes a certain degree of guts, strength, and effort.

Being gracious allows you to remain in a position of power. When you are gracious (especially when the other person does not deserve it), you are being benevolent. A person may not deserve the graciousness you afford them, but you, in your magnanimity, give it anyway.

Remember: you reap what you sow. If I go on the offensive, being rude and critical about the shortcomings of others' books, then I invite other people to do the same to mine. While I certainly welcome constructive criticism, I would appreciate it if it wasn't public.

Being gracious is a signal of maturity, confidence, and professionalism. To me, it's the opposite of making a crude joke in a professional setting. If you do, it shows that you still have a ways to go—that you're lacking some needed personal and professional development. Until you reach that, you're not ready to be invited into "the know."

Another reason to be gracious is so that later you will not look like an idiot. As I get older, I find that I am more confident in myself and my abilities. At the same time, I am more aware of how nuanced life is. Old criticisms I used to make no longer seem so smart. Life is not black and white, but a little of both with a lot of gray. After I started writing and ghostwriting business books, I had a lot more sympathy and fewer gripes about other authors' mistakes. Had I put some of those previous scathing criticisms in print, I would feel like a fool now.

I do not like to use counterexamples when I write. I would rather show you someone who did it right versus someone who did it wrong. But for specificity's sake, sometimes I have to use an example of doing it wrong. When I do, I try to be as kind as I can. Instead of railing about the stupidity, ignorance, and incompetence of someone else, I humbly offer my opinion and objectively focus on why I disagree with their approach.

On my blog, I occasionally post about a great book I read. More often, I focus on a key aspect of it. I could blog every day about what I find wrong in an author's book. It takes a lot more effort to find what's right.

Anyone can be critical. It's a lot harder to be creative.

STAY POSITIVE

"If you're not having fun, you're doing something wrong."
~ GROUCHO MARX

Author-artist Julia Cameron writes wonderful books to encourage poets, writers, sculptors, playwrights, and the like. Despite her target audience, I recommend her books to everyone. Julia talks about art, but what she addresses is life. You'll be hard-pressed to find a better personal development book.[3]

Julia introduced me to the concept of "drama tornadoes"—the people in our lives who always seem to be at the center of a whirlwind of drama and tragedy (and we all have them). As their friends and loved ones, we try to help them, yet are inevitably sucked into their soap opera. Intentionally or not, these drama whirlwinds steal our peace, optimism, and energy, leaving us as stressed out and frustrated as they are (or worse). They come in different sizes, shapes, and packages, but they all have the same ultimate effect.

Albert Bernstein coined the phrase "emotional vampire" to underscore how these types seem to suck the life right out of us. When we leave their presence, we rub our necks to find the puncture marks. Who wants to be around people like that? No one in their right mind, of course.

So, ask yourself this question: who wants to buy books that make them feel like that? If that's your reader, go right ahead. But if you want a bestseller, you have to keep the tone of your book positive and upbeat.

---

[3] This is a perfect example of what we discussed in chapter three: just because you write for one audience doesn't mean that other people won't find, read, and love your book.

You may have an axe to grind. Maybe thirty years of slogging through the proverbial mud has left you bitter. You're jaded. Life isn't the bed of roses you thought it would be. By all means, get all of that out of your system and onto paper.

Just don't put it in your book.

When you step "on stage," you need to make people feel better about themselves. They don't want to hear your gripes. They want to hear how you can solve their problems, earn them a million bucks, and make them look ten years younger to boot.

Go look at the best-selling business books. It is rare to find a doom-and-gloom one sitting on the shelves. The best authors generally have a hopeful, inspiring, uplifting, or forward-looking tone. You do not need to be a circus promoter. You don't even have to be cheery. Just be positive.

This goes for not just your tone, but your very word choice. Consider:

> *Michael is incapable of writing a book that isn't imaginative and intelligent.*

I happened to see that on the front cover of a book in Barnes and Noble. I had to read it twice to get what the reviewer meant. Because he phrased it as a negative (that the author is incapable of doing something), the reviewer disguised his praise under the veil of a double negative (he can't *not* write well).

The content of the review is high praise, indeed, but the delivery got in the way because of the author's use of a double negative.

Here is a side-by-side example. Hone in on the last few words:

Negative	Positive
Less than 10 percent of all jobs are filled through online posts and the ones that are usually aren't the best types.	*Less than 10 percent of all jobs are filled through online posts and the ones that are usually are the low-end types.*

Yes, this is a subtle difference, but one sounds slightly judgmental and pessimistic while the other states an unfortunate fact in a neutral tone. Now, imagine a whole paragraph written in this subtly judgmental tone. Then a section. Then a chapter. Then an entire manuscript. The negativity would accumulate and compound until the entire book became a dreary dredge of disparate dirges.[4]

People naturally gravitate towards positivity. There is plenty of depressing news going around. Don't add to the world's burden. Be a beacon of hope and light in a dreary, desperate existence.

No Jargon, Consultese, or TLAs

> *"'Benchmarked against best-in-class peers, intellectual capital leverage reveals significant upward potential moving forward.' What it really means: Companies like yours make better use of their employees' knowledge."*
> ~ Jamie Whyte, *Bad Thoughts: A Guide to Clear Thinking*

If you write an article for a niche trade journal or publish a white paper, you can use all the industry technical jargon you like.

If you're in a meeting with a client and feel the need to dazzle them with your linguistic mastery of consultese, then quote the above.

If you're writing a business book, then any high school student should be able to pick it up and follow along.

It does not matter if your reader has a PhD in data analytics. When you write a business book, it must be appropriate for the business trade audience—and the business trade audience sets the bar at about high school English. Aim for that reading level and assume nothing.

Believe it or not, plenty of successful businesspeople around the world trip on the TLA KPI thrown into the middle of a sentence. They

---

[4] Dr. Seuss, eat your heart out.

have almost assuredly run across it before, but it is not something many use on a daily basis. If you do use a TLA, make sure you define it the first time you use it.[5]

Do not assume that people use the same industry-specific vocabulary you do, even in your same industry. With my data analytics authors, I learned that Walmart refers to its product shelving design as a "modular" while most other retailers refer to it as a "planogram." Most retailers refer to their customers as customers, but Target uses the word "guests."

Sometimes your readers may be students or newcomers. Some people don't speak English as a native language. In the increasingly global economy, the market for business books is wider than ever. Writing above a high school reading level makes it difficult for them to slog through your book. In all likelihood, they will put it down. Plus, it is just plain rude to expect your reader to be as well-versed in your field as you are.

Authority in writing is derived from the clarity and brilliance of your ideas—not by how well you have mastered the dictionary and the thesaurus.

THE UNFORGIVABLE SIN

"Always remember that you are absolutely unique. Just like everyone else."
~ ATTRIBUTED TO MARGARET MEAD

A normal corporate mission might go something like, "We will deliver extreme customer satisfaction, foster an environment our associates love to work in, and create extraordinary value for our shareholders."

(In fact, that may even be a little edgy for big companies since I used the words "extreme" and "love.")

From this ubiquitous statement, we cannot even tell what industry the company is in, much less what the company's purpose is. No one can cite it word for word. No one remembers it. No one cares about it.

---

[5] ...as I have purposely not done here. Unless you know what TLA stands for, you feel left behind.

In *The Art of the Start*, Guy Kawasaki attacks such bland mission statements. To show what they should look like, he suggests memorable mantras for existing companies and organizations that everyone could remember and use as a rallying cry:

+ Wendy's: "Healthy fast food."[6]

+ FedEx: "Peace of mind."

+ Southwest Airlines: "Better than driving."

+ March of Dimes: "Save babies."

…and my personal favorite:

+ US Air Force: "Kick a** in air and space."

It's been at least six years since I read Kawasaki's book, so I did have to look up the other mantras, but I had no trouble remembering his mantra for the Air Force.

Did you get that? Six *years* later I quickly recalled a mantra that does not even exist. That, my friend, is memorable writing.

In working with business authors, I have had clients who didn't care for the degree of edginess I suggested and wanted me to tone it down. I love my clients and respect their opinion (and, at the end of the day, they're the boss), so of course I changed it. While it might have resulted in a more conventional read, usually it gets so normal as to be unmemorable.

I encourage you to take a risk and go out on a limb. Your clients and audience need to remember what they read, and if you have to color outside the lines a little to achieve that, it may well be worth it.

When I read books, I'm okay with an unpolished presentation. We're all busy, things get overlooked, and maybe the author did not have the right professional help. I can forgive bad English and punctuation

---

[6] I think "healthy" is a bit of a stretch, but that's what Kawasaki suggested.

mistakes. It's a hard language and no one's perfect. I'll even let you slide on saying some of the same things everyone else does. There are only so many original ideas in the world.

But I cannot forgive bland, pasty, generic, crumbly, mealy-mouthed, forgettable writing. The whole point of authoring a book is to convey information, compelling people towards some end or another. If no one remembers what you write, then—really—why bother?

In *Anne of Green Gables*, Anne's foster mother adopts two children, Dora and Davy. Dora is obedient, proper, and no trouble at all. Davy is her opposite: always in trouble, always in some kind of scrape, and always a source of worry. Secretly, Anne likes Davy more because he is so much more fun. His character in the book is memorable. Dora, on the other hand, is utterly forgettable.

Don't be a Dora, playing it safe. Be adventurous. Be memorable. Be Davy.

NEWFANGLED TECHNOLOGY

> *"A society grows great when old men plant trees whose shade they know they shall never sit in."*
> ~ GREEK PROVERB

Don't you find it quaint when you read older business books that say, "Write to the address below for a FREE CD-ROM!"

Or even older ones: "If you send a self-addressed, stamped envelope to the address below, the author will send you a FREE 3.5" floppy disk!"

This, from books published in the 1990s—not really that long ago. (Well, at least not to me.)

The respective authors were in rightful awe of the wonders of then-modern technology. When I read this in the middle of a great business book, though, it jolts me into remembering that the book is several years old—decades, some cases. Fax machines came and went. (Okay, they're dying a slow and begrudging death.) Do they still make discs for CD-ROMs anymore? The internet and email are, of course, still here, but they're not the new and revolutionary media they were once considered. Today, they're just like telephones and staplers—a fixture in business.

To be blunt, the reference dates their book.

While the content around much of these passages remains as relevant as ever, the specific references to technology diminishes the respect and perceived authority I have for their words. As a business author writing a book that's going to be around for at least five years—if not fifteen or twenty—these things matter. Plenty of business gurus have been (or were) around for that long: Zig Ziglar, Stephen Covey, Jim Collins, Tom Peters, John Maxwell, Dan Kennedy, Malcolm Gladwell, and Jack Canfield, just to name a few.

On the other hand, let me show you how powerful this can be when you do it right. A colleague of mine came across a copy of *Blue Ocean Strategy* and thought it was so spot-on that he wanted to buy a copy for a friend of his. He went online and couldn't find it at the major retailers. Finally, he looked at the copyright page and was surprised to find that it had been published almost a decade before. Without any clues in the content as to its publication date, he thought it was a recent book.

Blue Ocean Strategy could get around technology references. However, there are some places where it's almost impossible (although even these will probably fall into the dustbin of history soon enough). For example, I almost can't write about books and publishing without referring to Amazon at some point. Facebook, Google, and Twitter are also too big to ignore. AOL used to be in this category, but many people in my generation do not even remember America Online. Professionals just five years younger than me have never even heard the enchanting music of a dial-up modem. The iPhone is ubiquitous enough now, but a few years ago you could have said that about BlackBerrys.

Even by writing this, I am ignoring my own advice and dating this manuscript with such references. However, the degree of specificity this allows (that is, using concrete examples, per my earlier advice) outweighs the consequences.

I am not giving you a list of what tech pieces you can use or not. In writing a book, I simply caution you to be aware of how quickly technology changes and how much quicker that pace has become.

If your book is about how to use a technology, then absolutely use it—but as soon as you finish, be ready to write another. Your book will be obsolete shortly. If your book has a story or example that uses a technology (one of my clients refers to a number of customer relationship management applications she implemented), by all means use it—just be aware that it dates your story, if not your book.

For referencing technology outside of such content or stories, the best alternative is to relegate all such references to a resources page or simply just the very last pages of your book. In business books I have from the 70s, 80s, and 90s, it seems like all of them have offers at the end of some chapters. I can write, call, or email for more information. Today, I rarely see authors inserting an actual mailing address anywhere in the book, much less in the content.

Addresses, websites, and other external references properly go in a dedicated "resources" or "for further reading" section, or in an order form at the end. Depending on the length, you could also put it on the front or back cover. That way, when you reprint your book or release a new edition, you can just update the cover and/or those last two or three pages without having to redesign the whole interior—a costly and time-consuming affair.

But, honestly, if your reader wants more information, don't you imagine they'll just go search for it with whatever means are at their disposal? If they lived back in the Stone Age, they could go to their library. Today, they can do an internet search (notice I did not say "a Google search"). Tomorrow, we may all have holographic personal assistants who do our virtual errands for us. Who knows?

Don't worry about getting with the times. Craft a manuscript that will stand the test of time.

FORESHADOWING

> *"Telling someone what's going to happen later is called 'foreshadowing.' Foreshadowing is appropriate only in fiction."*
> ~ CLAUDIA SUZANNE

The ol' tried-and-true format to public speaking is:

1. Tell 'em what you're going to tell 'em.
2. Tell 'em.
3. Tell 'em what you told 'em.

That works in presentations and seminars where you're trying to hold your audience's attention. You have to compete with the clock, that guy in the third row sneezing and hacking every thirty seconds, and with the extra-grande latte they chugged down right before you began. With books, the pace is different. Your audience of one chooses the pace at which they read. If there's a demand on their time, they can put the book down and come back later.

That's why it's unnecessary (even distracting within the context of the book itself) to tell 'em what you're going to tell 'em. For example: "In a later chapter, I'm going to explain this, but let me go ahead and say it right now," or, "We'll talk more about this later, but for now…"

As Claudia's quote said, foreshadowing is for fiction. In fiction, the reader weaves a whole other reality as they read. They are *there*. In a well-written novel, the reader is swept along with the current, flowing with the plot and characters. Because they passively move through the story, it's okay when the crazy old man on the side of the road gives the hero an ominous warning with a glaring eye. The reader thinks, *Hmmm, I wonder what that means? Will our beloved hero fall prey to the siren call and never complete his quest?* They enjoy the mystery and look forward to solving the puzzle.

You do not want to foreshadow in business books. It takes considerably more effort to achieve a state of flow with nonfiction. People do not read business books for a sense of mystery and they do not eagerly look forward to the resolution of questions raised chapters before. They buy them primarily to solve a problem—and they want the answer now.

When you do achieve that flow where the reader is smoothly led from one logical point to another, you interrupt their train of thought by essentially saying, "I know you've been focusing here, but instead of leading you to my next point, let me say you need to put a mental pin in this discussion because we're going to return to it in a little while. Going back to the matter at hand, though…"

Teasing or simply telling the business reader what's to come sometimes annoys or even frustrates them. By raising the issue, you potentially raise other questions, such as, *Well why didn't he go ahead and explain it right here? Why do I have to wait? What isn't he telling me about it now?*

I won't lie: I've been tempted to do the same thing with a number of my authors' books. In one chapter we introduced their concept, but didn't want to overwhelm the reader. We provided the explanation in measured degrees, one piece at a time. At the same time, we were afraid the reader might feel that the author didn't know what he was talking about, that the author hadn't satisfactorily addressed an issue, or that the reader might get bored. Telling them what was ahead seemed like an easy way to signal that the author knew a lot more than what they said in one particular section.

It's almost like those cheesy infomercials where at the end of selling the product, they say, "But wait—there's more!"

You don't want any part of your book to be the literary equivalent of that. If you do your job right, you won't have to worry about people putting your book down or being so bored that they toss it completely.

As with everything else, there are exceptions. Foretelling properly finds a home anywhere in the front matter, such as the preface, introduction, or foreword. There, people expect you to tell them what's to come.

Transitions also bend this rule. As a matter of style and interest, you can say what the reader will find in the next chapter—but only at the end of the current one. Even in this case, it's not so much about saying what's to come as it is a cliffhanger—the introduction to the next chapter that comes just a few sentences on this side of the page break. You can raise a question at the end of one section if you immediately answer it in the next.

All of this advice ties back into my previous warning: don't write defensively. Don't write with the constant fear that people will think your book is boring, irrelevant, or shallow. Write proudly, confident in the fact you have a great book.

Don't say what you're going to do. Just do it.

"I Don't Have Time to Address This Right Now..."

"I love deadlines. I like the whooshing sound they make as they fly by."
~ Douglas Adams

There is something worse than referring to material that's to come later: referring to material that won't come later.

Have you ever been in a seminar where the presenter says, "We don't have time to go into that right now, but—" and keeps going? Or perhaps a university lecture where the professor kept referring to all the other topics related to the presentation, but never took the time to address them because they had to finish their spiel for that class?

It makes me feel breathless, as if I am being bombarded with too much information to process.

A presentation should be tight, focused, and exciting. The presenter should be calm, cool, and collected. Continually referring to things off-topic tells me that either they are unprepared for this particular lecture, they do not know how to structure their thoughts, or they feel the need to impress me. In any of these cases, I lose interest. I did not attend the event because I wanted an overview of the entire discipline or field of study; I just wanted to learn what I came to learn.

So you can imagine how I feel about authors who do this in their books. If you do not have time to talk about something...don't. If your book is not about a tangential subject, keep it that way. I lose respect for authors for the same reasons: it makes me question how prepared they were, how focused their book is, and why they feel the need to impress me with how many other books and white papers they've read.

Instead of saying that "Space doesn't permit me to expound on this topic, but—" or "We don't have time to delve into that, but—" why not put a list of recommended reading at the back of your book? Or you could put a list of recommended sources at the end of each chapter. Or, if you prefer, you could mark it for an endnote, as so many academic-leaning books do. Or better yet, create a dynamic resource that you can update.

That way, people who want more on one specific idea have the option to do so, but the rest of us can continue on without having to read the equivalent of you trying to plow through sixty presentation slides in five minutes, shouting, "I don't have time to tell you about this, but it's really interesting!"

WRITE SOUND BITES

*"Business authors don't count on their book's sales—
they count on what their book sells."*
~ DEREK LEWIS, *THE BUSINESS BOOK BIBLE*

I love quotes. I collect them wherever I can and share them in books and social media. But some business books make it hard for me. While their authors are brilliant and offer great ideas, they rarely offer a good sound bite I can use. I sometimes cobble something together with a lot of brackets and ellipses, but then it looks more like a "Frankenquote."

A good sound bite makes it easy for a journalist, a reviewer, an interviewer, a blogger, and everyone else to quote you in their own work or at an event. A plethora of good sound bites also makes it more likely that you'll be quoted—in a manager's meeting, in another author's book, in a company's newsletter, and all over the internet. The easier you make it for other people to find snippets, the more likely it is that they'll use them.

In fact, some people are probably going to attempt to sum up your book in a just a few sentences anyway. By giving them a gem of a quote, you can, to a degree, control the outcome. Otherwise, you leave it in their incapable hands. (After all, who knows your material better than you?)

When you go back through the editing phase, pepper sound bites throughout your content. One way is to attempt to summarize an entire section or chapter in one punchy sentence. Then, you can place that somewhere in that section or chapter. Putting it at the end is particularly effective, or you could offer a summary at the conclusion of a chapter.

Make it easy for people to quote your brilliance.

EDIT. REVISE. REPEAT.

"Remember, it is no sign of weakness or defeat that your manuscript ends up in need of major surgery. This is a common occurrence in all writing, and among the best writers."
~ WILLIAM STRUNK JR., *THE ELEMENTS OF STYLE*

"Everyone knows it takes a woman nine months to have a baby. But you Americans think if you get nine women pregnant, you can have a baby in a month."
~ THEODORE VON KÁRMÁN

"Six months to write a book! I could almost have a baby in that time!" Judging by his words and tone, this potential client was genuinely shocked that I said it would take six to seven months to ghostwrite the book he had just described. I don't know why he was so surprised. Just figuring out what to say in the first place is an arduous process. Then, rearranging, editing, polishing, and refining is a whole other endeavor.

Some clients approach me with a manuscript "about half-finished." What they really mean is that they are half-finished with the first draft. That is a long way from being done with the finished draft. There are rounds and rounds of in-depth reading, thinking, critiquing, analyzing, and editing to go through before the end is even in sight. Getting a book ready to present to the market takes a lot of hard work.

You need to read through it on your computer. Fix the things you can and mark where things seem awkward or just not quite right. Then print it out on paper and read through it again, marking it up as you go. Go back and revise it. Then get your spouse, peers, and colleagues to read through chapters (or, if they're up to it, the whole thing), asking them to mark it up as they go. Let them tell you how ugly your baby is, as much you hate to hear it. Take their ideas into consideration, revising as you see fit.

Then print it out and read it again.

Separate the nice-to-know from the need-to-know. Buttress the latter; lay the former to rest. Perform major surgery, gutting this part here and reattaching it over there. Don the plastic surgeon's mask and rework the cosmetics of whole sections. Put on your dentist's hat and extract the cavities while polishing the healthy.

Lather. Rinse. Repeat.

HOW LONG WILL IT TAKE? (PART II)

"Better a diamond with a flaw than a pebble without one."
~ CHINESE PROVERB

I know my obsessive-compulsive readers may faint dead away upon reading the following statement, and that it may seem to contradict what I just wrote. Nevertheless, it must be said.

Your book will be never perfect.

In chapter one, I told you that regardless of how long it takes, you must commit yourself to writing a great book. Now I have to tell you not to take too long to do it.

I could take another ten years to publish this book and it would be much better for the wait. But that would not help those would-be authors like you who need to know—*right now*—what I know. More importantly for me, my manuscript is of absolutely no use to my business sitting on my hard drive, waiting until it is perfect before I release it.

Good enough is good enough.

But what is good enough? The best I have ever heard it summed up was in a quote by Antoine de Saint-Exupéry: "A designer knows he has achieved perfection not when there is nothing left to add, but when there is nothing left to take away."

In modern business parlance, this is a "minimum viable product": the least developed product a company can release that meets minimum market expectations. With a business book, that means releasing a book that looks, feels, and reads like a professionally prepared book. (Anything less is a "galley copy" or simply a "draft.") Moreover, it needs to make good on its promise: it must provide enough information to either solve your reader's problem or equip them to the point they feel they are ready to tackle it.

Your reader should be able to turn the last page and feel satisfied. They should feel that they took something away and that they are better for having read it.

Sound Bite Summary

- Writing is about knowing what to say. Editing is about knowing how to say it.

- Edit your writing until it's so smooth the reader forgets they're even reading.

- Writing a business book is more like bringing life to Frankenstein than painting the Mona Lisa.

- Don't apologize for your book.

- When you write your book, be gracious.

- Anyone can be a critic. It's a lot harder to be creative.

✦ The world has enough negativity. Stay positive.

✦ Write business books for a high-school reading level.

✦ Authority in writing comes from the clarity and brilliance of your thoughts—not by how well you've mastered the dictionary.

✦ If you want people to remember your book, make it memorable.

✦ Don't worry about getting with the times. Craft a manuscript that will stand the test of time.

✦ Good enough is good enough.

9

WHAT SHOULD
I TITLE IT?

*"Choose a title for your book at least as carefully as you
would select a given name for your firstborn child."*
~ NAT BODIAN, *HOW TO CHOOSE A WINNING TITLE*

N AT GOT IT RIGHT.

With both of our children, my wife and I discussed names for
hours on end. There are entire websites and even books devoted to the
task of picking out a baby name. If you've ever attempted to go through
this with your own significant other, you know how emotional, exciting,
and stressful it can be.

Names are important. To a degree, they define us. Whether because
of some inherent quality or because of how people treat certain names,
our own can shape who we become. We expect a "John" to be dependable. A "Catherine" might be demure. A boy named Sue has to be a
tough son-of-a-gun.

Sure, a baby's name is important—but a book's name? Does it
really make or break the book? Isn't it really just a roll of the dice? And

doesn't the author's reputation and marketing strategy matter more anyway? I mean, when you go to the bookstore, the titles of successful business books run the gamut, from the utilitarian (*How to Win Friends and Influence People*) to the intriguing (*Who Moved My Cheese?*) to the obscure (*Purple Cow*).

I can't teach you how to write a title that will guarantee success. What I can tell you is how I have applied my expertise from working with a couple dozen manuscripts, my experience from having read a few hundred business books, my naturally critical eye, and some serious thought to develop some insights into what you should aim for.

WHY TAKE THE TIME TO WRITE A KILLER TITLE

> *"There are book titles that deserve better books, and there are books that deserve better titles."*
> ~ DAN POYNTER, *WRITING NONFICTION*

Is a title important?

Absolutely.

In fact, it's critical. It's the first impression people have of your book. If they never get any further than the title, then it doesn't matter how great of a book you wrote—they'll never stick around long enough to find out. On the other hand, plenty of people make the decision to buy a book based solely on reading the title. The classic *Think and Grow Rich* is one such example; *The One Minute Manager* is another. Plenty of people have bought both just because of the promise or solution implied.

So, yes: an effective title can propel your book to success or doom it to relative failure.

Other books succeed *in spite of* their titles. Let's establish one profound truth about business book titles: a successful book is not the same thing as a successful title. As Dan Poynter's quote notes, great books and great titles don't always go hand in hand.

Then again, some books' success has nothing to do with how effective or ineffective their title is. Seth Godin can name his next book whatever he wants to and it will sell on the strength of his reputation alone. Everything he's written thus far has held nuggets of wisdom and we expect his next will be no less. Malcolm Gladwell, too: *Blink* and *Outliers* sound more like sci-fi action thrillers than science-based insights on life. But with Gladwell's name on the cover, they will fly off the shelves.[1]

But unless you are an established author like Godin or Gladwell, you can't count on the strength of your name to carry your book. In fact, you need to write effective business titles even if you have a great marketing platform like these guys. That way, you can still appeal to people who have never heard of you.

Trump and *Iacocca* would be great examples of books that sold off the strength of their titles alone…if the titles did not tie right back into the idea of people buying the book because they recognize the name. Again, even if you're a famous celebrity, you should write a title that can attract a completely new audience.

We could use *Financial Peace* as an example. The title taps into one of the biggest sources of emotional (and marital) turmoil, plus implies a solution in the same breath. But you could argue that Dave Ramsey had a ready market for his book through his personal finance company.

With all these examples, the success of the authors' books may have been unrelated to their titles. To prove my point about the importance of a great title, we need an unknown person with no established market where the business book became a bestseller on the strength of its title alone.

Cue *The 4-Hour Workweek*.

Tim Ferris enjoyed record sales and earned a cult following because he shared life-changing insights in his book—but it all started with the spark of his killer title. (In fact, the story of how he finally settled on that

---

[1] These two authors write books that are perfect examples of what I continually preach: a great business book should be both insightful and interesting. That is, it must deliver substantial value in a compelling way.

title inside his book is an informative read in itself.) He took the time to nail down the words on the cover. That's what propelled his book's success and launched him onto the international stage.

Nat was right: pick out your book's name as carefully as you would your own kid's.[2]

WHAT YOUR TITLE IS SUPPOSED TO DO

> *"Authors, as a rule, are poor judges of titles and often go for the cute or clever rather than the practical."*
> ~ NAT BODIAN, *HOW TO CHOOSE A WINNING TITLE*

Before we can begin to judge what a good business book title really is, we must first agree on what it's supposed to do.

An effective title can sell the book on its strength alone.

Before your reader will buy, you have to capture their attention. Before you can capture their attention, you have to capture their eye.

Have you ever used microfilm to search through old newspapers or library collections? The negative images of the papers zoom by in a blur. All you can do is get the gist of the big-lettered headlines. When one catches your eye, you stop and then click on the backlight that turns the negative image into a normal one so you can read the rest of the story.

That's what your title has to do. While your potential reader is zooming through their everyday life, your title has to catch their eye so that they stop and the light clicks on: "Oh! That looks interesting!" Subconsciously, they began to ask, "I wonder if this book solves a problem I have. I wonder if it will meet my expectations. I wonder if it's what I've been looking for."

From looking at your title, your prospective reader will usually look at your subtitle, then whatever other copy is on the front (blurb, "Foreword by," etc.), and then turn it over to read the back and/or dust jacket copy. If they are online, they follow a similar process: they start

---

[2] Although, and ironically, Nat's own title could have been better.

by looking at your cover and title, then read the subtitle, and then read the rest of the content on the page.

The task of selling your book is a more intricate matter than it generally appears, although the actual decision of buying your book may happen in just a matter of seconds. In any event, it starts with your title.[3]

But a *great* title can sell your book all by itself.

So how do you successfully capture your intended audience's attention? Do you signal specifically who the book's for, such as *HR Managers: Read This Book*? Do you use an unusual title to arouse their curiosity, à la *Meatball Sundae*? Do you go with something as straightforward as *How to Get a Job As a Coder*? All these approaches have apparently worked over the years for their respective authors. So which one works best?

There's no one single factor; there are actually five. They form a ladder of importance. You have to address one rung before you can proceed to the next—something like Maslow's hierarchy of needs. I call it the 5 Cs. A great business book title is:

1. Clear
2. Compelling
3. Convenient
4. Clever
5. Continuous

If you have to choose between being clear and being clever, err on the side of clarity. If you have to choose between a title that provokes a response or one that is easy to remember, go for the action. Don't fall so in love with one particular title that you skip over more important considerations. Too many authors discover too late that "an ounce of prevention is worth a pound of cure."

Get it right.

---

[3] Actually, your reader's first impression is a combination of your cover and title, which is why "Thou Shalt Not Skimp On Thy Cover" is number one on my list of "The 7 Deadly Sins of Business Books."

#1: BE CLEAR

> *"A great title must say what it is."*
> ~ BLAKE SNYDER, *SAVE THE CAT!*

Everyone wants an awesome title—one that they can throw out at parties and immediately see their listeners' eyes shine with interest: "Wow, that sounds so cool!" Trust me: we all want that moment.

Unfortunately, nearly zero business books are sold at dinner parties. Impressive titles might sound like music to your ears. But when the lonely solitary executive is running through the airport or the time-pressed small business owner has a two-minute break to scroll through Amazon's book list on her smartphone, they don't hear the same music you do. All they hear is yet more white noise in their already overcrowded day trying to intrude on what precious little attention they have to give to any one thing.

They aren't looking for "cute."

As we discussed before, in *The 100 Best Business Books of All Time* the authors said, "The number one reason people buy business books is to find solutions to problems." A good title speaks to the problem the book solves. Use your title to speak to (or at least hint at) their problem. Identify their position, their industry, and/or exactly what they're facing. Put something in the title that calls out to them. (I mean, you can't even tell some business books are intended for a business audience, just going by the title.)

Don't be ambiguous—clearly signal that this book is what they've been looking for. *Getting Things DONE* doesn't capture your imagination, though it certainly captures your attention (if you're pressed for time—and who isn't?). *Writing Nonfiction* won't win any awards for creativity, but for writers like me, the title alone is enough to persuade me to take a serious look at buying it. *What Makes the Great Great?* strikes you as an odd question...but there's no question on its content.

The opposite of being clear is being obscure. Obscure titles fall under the broad heading of "I have no idea what this book is about from just reading the title." Do you really want your book's success to rely on someone taking the additional time and effort to pick up your book, read the rest of the front and back cover copy, process everything, and then finally figure out that your book is what they need?

Good luck with that.

Your title needs to shout its relevance to your reader. You, the author, know where they, the reader, live. You know what keeps them up at night. You know their reality. You know their address.

Make sure they know you know that.

#2: BE COMPELLING

"Make your readers want to cheer your name or make them want to tear you limb from limb, but never let them be bored."
~ ERIC RHOADS

By "compelling," I mean tap into the psyche of your reader.

You could do this by making or implying a promise or solution. You could elicit an emotional response or a subconscious appeal. At the very least, it should be interesting enough to make them want to take a closer look. While the titles of *The Wealthy Freelancer* and *The Well-Fed Writer* would never pull people in to see the movie, they are compelling to their target market nonetheless.

(Believe me, as a starving copywriter for a couple of years, both of those titles are extremely intriguing.)

Financial Peace, too, accomplishes this by implying the desired feeling (calm) about a fear-inducing subject (money). The two writing authors could have said something like *How to Make More Money Writing*; Dave Ramsey could have called his book *How to Save More Money*. While those titles clearly identify their audiences and their problems, they aren't nearly as compelling as the ones they finally settled on.

Priority #1 establishes the "what" of the book. Priority #2 should establish the "why": *why* should your audience buy the book? What compelling word or sentiment is in there that would move them to action?

#3: BE CONVENIENT

"I would have written a shorter letter, but I did not have the time."
~ BLAISE PASCAL, *PROVINCIAL LETTERS: LETTER XVI*

Successful titles are easy to recall. If someone is recommending a book, they can probably remember the title easily, since they invested some time and thought into it. The convenience factor in naming your book is really for people who hear of your book in passing—listening to the radio or the news, reading about it in a magazine or newsletter, or while talking to a friend. If the book's subject or recommendation piques their interest, and they later want to find it at the bookstore or online, you want to make it as easy as possible to help them remember it.

Using the least number of words is one easy way; *Influence* comes to mind. The fewer words people have to remember, the more likely it is they'll be able to do so. *Good to Great* and *Built to Last* are succinct and punchy enough to easily recall, even if you haven't read them. Another successful triple-syllable title lands here, too: *It's Your Ship*.

Mnemonics[4] work well, as with the rhyming of *Quest for the Best*. Despite its age, it's still one of my all-time favorites as a title and a business book. *Why We Buy* is beautiful example of a title that is clear, compelling, and convenient, both short and rhyming—just like *The Art of the Start*. Besides being succinct, *Good to Great* is a classic example of an alliterative title, as are *The Fred Factor*, *Selling Sunshine*, and *The Go-Giver*.

What Got You Here Won't Get You There is a mouthful, but it works because it easily rolls off the tongue. The rhythmic *ba-BUM-ba-BUM-ba-BUM-ba-BUM* combined with the simple imagery of getting from point A to point B make the title effective.

---

[4] Whose cruel idea was it to stick an M at the beginning of that word?

A little wordsmithing made all of these examples easy to say and easy to remember.

You can also play off well-known phrases or easy-to-recall questions. *What Would Google Do?* is a twist on the oft used "what would _____ do?" dating back to as early as 1897. *What Is Your ONE Sentence?* works because we think about the infamous elevator speech we're all supposed to have handy for that one time we ride from one floor to another with the billionaire investor who gives us his undivided attention.

Convenience goes beyond being easy to remember. Your title needs to be easy to find, too. Weird punctuation, using words often misspelled, or using made-up words can trip up your would-be reader (or a clerk at the bookstore trying to order for your reader). One of my authors toyed with the idea of combining the words "success" and "execution" as a kind of trademark to build his platform around. But it did not take us very long to look at *SuXeXecution* (and variations thereof) to completely abandon the idea.

He got an A for originality, but if no one could spell the title, the market would grade it with an F.

#4: BE CLEVER

> *"Don't tell me the moon is shining; show me*
> *the glint of light on broken glass."*
> ~ ANTON CHEKOV

You can write a clever title—*if* your audience and/or problem is signaled, *if* you offer a compelling reason to read the book, and *if* it's easy to remember. Then and only then is it okay to use a cute or clever title that impresses the locals.

Clever titles are great. They win not just attention and interest but add a bit of intrigue to the book—that is, they amplify what you accomplished in the first three Cs. *The Warren Buffet Way* makes the list. Without referring to investing or financial planning in any way, the author cleverly alludes to it while piquing the reader's interest. ("I'd love to invest like the Oracle of Omaha!")

Dave Ramsey's *EntreLeadership* accomplishes this in one fell swoop. With a clever combination of "entrepreneurship" and "leadership," Dave identifies the who and what (entrepreneurs who need help being effective leaders). Moreover, he also deserves kudos for having an intriguing title. Brilliant.

Other authors have coined their own words in their respective titles to hit the cleverness factor, too. *Locavesting* is a smart title, combining locavore plus "investing." For anyone familiar with the go local theme, it instantly says that it's about investing in your local economy. *Rework* gets high marks for being succinct while also signaling its subject (rethinking how we work). *Freakonomics* works, too, as my mind makes the leap from "freak" to "Frankenstein." Combine that image with economics and you'll hook a geek like me every time.

Clever turns of phrase work well, too. *The Wizard of Ads* gets high points for identifying its contents (marketing) while calling Dorothy and Toto to mind. *The War of Art* is a neat twist on the well-known *Art of War* while at the same time giving you a clue that it's about the struggles of being an artist. While *Eat That Frog* ranks low on the self-identification factor, it is a clear winner in the hard-to-forget category. *The Small-Mart Revolution*, a book on small businesses facing off against big box retailers, is a great play off Walmart, identifying its contents and associating it with the world's biggest business.

Then again, some titles are so spot-on that they are clever. *Your Marketing Sucks.* may be one of the best business titles ever: clear, compelling, succinct, and intriguing. Then, too, we must consider *The 4-Hour Workweek* again. Its premise alone is enough to make the cut.

#5: BE CONTINUOUS

"Begin as you mean to go on."
- CHARLES H. SPURGEON, *ALL OF GRACE*

It is nigh impossible to hit all four of those milestones and still shoulder on to the Holy Grail of killer business book titles: one that lends itself to a series. But if you can and do, then each subsequent book will enjoy the compound interest[5] of its predecessors (and vice versa).

Dan Kennedy's *No B.S.* title falls squarely in the "lends itself to a series category" (by smart design, not happy accident; Dan is brilliant): *No B.S. Marketing to the Affluent*, *No B.S. Price Strategy Guide*, and *No B.S. Ruthless Management of People and Profits*, among many others.

Although I wouldn't put a check mark in its "clever" category, *The One Minute Manager* is a great example of a title that can be easily reconfigured for subsequent titles. Unsurprisingly, Ken Blanchard did just that, with *The One Minute Entrepreneur*, *The One Minute Manager Meets the Monkey*, *How a "Last-Minute Manager" Conquered Procrastination*[6], and other derivatives.

Rich Dad, Poor Dad spawned a whole *Rich Dad* series on real estate, sales professionals, legal entities, and more. Michael Gerber has successfully used *The E-Myth* in a number of other small business-related volumes. Yet again, *The 4-Hour Workweek* shows up as a great example of being contiguous. Ever the entrepreneur, Tim Ferris parlayed the success of his book into *The 4-Hour Body* and *The 4-Hour Chef*.

Here, too, we have another appearance of *Your Marketing Sucks*. It's easy to imagine a whole series of *Your _____ Sucks*. It just lends itself to that kind of wordplay. Wisely, Mark Stevens took advantage of it, subsequently writing *Your Company Sucks.* and *Your Management Sucks.* There are plenty of other titles that haven't been used for additional books, but you could imagine them. I could easily see Dave Ramsey leveraging *EntreLeadership* in *EntreManagement* and *EntreFinance*, for example.

---

[5] Yes, that was a horrible pun.

[6] This last example is actually the subtitle to his book *The On-Time, On-Target Manager*. I might have suggested simply going with *The Last-Minute Manager,* then write the subtitle as *How to Conquer Procrastination and Become an On-Time, On-Target Manager* to play off the strength of the initial title.

If you can hit the first four Cs and still find a way to leave your title open for spinoffs, you are in a truly extraordinary league of authors.

THE SUBTITLE, YOUR TITLE'S WINGMAN

"Words are, of course, the most powerful drug used by mankind."
~ RUDYARD KIPLING

Every business book should have a subtitle.
Period.
Your title should do the heavy lifting in convincing your reader to buy the book. However, a subtitle gives you a second chance to fill in the gaps where your title didn't do its job.

Subtitles can be as long as you want and need them to be. The subtitle of one of Dan Kennedy's *No B.S.* books is *The Ultimate No Holds Barred Take No Prisoners Guide to Growing Sales and Profits of Local Small Businesses.* Eighteen words long—and that doesn't include the title.

If your title is clever but lacking in the clarity department, then your subtitle gives you the chance to clearly identify its contents and/or target audience. As I noted, *Eat That Frog* clearly makes the cut in creativity but we're left with no idea as to its subject. As such, that's what the subtitle has to accomplish, and Brian Tracy does so with this: *21 Ways to Stop Procrastinating and Get More Done in Less Time.* Clear and compelling.

On the other hand, if your book's title is utilitarian, you need a subtitle that makes it interesting. If your title is succinct, then the subtitle gives you the real estate to spread out. *The E-Myth* gets points for being short and sweet, but leaves no clue what the author is writing about. Ergo, its subtitle *Why Most Small Businesses Don't Work and What to Do About It* fills in the gap.

Some books are so tied to their subtitles that it is nearly impossible to separate them. *Trump: The Art of the Deal* and *Jack: Straight From the Gut* are two prime examples. Although *Trump* could perhaps stand on its own if it had to, *Jack* could not. Because the subtitle is an integral part of the title, I can't even bring myself to refer to it as just *Jack*. It doesn't even make sense.

But even though you can accomplish everything with a subtitle that you can with the title, a subtitle still carries the "sub" designation. That is, it's a secondary consideration. If you can't get your reader's attention with the title, then the subtitle will never have a chance.

But if you let your title do everything it should, then your subtitle can shift from supporting to amplifying. I identified *EntreLeadership* as a great business book title. Since it does everything it needs to, the author can use the subtitle to underscore his own experience with *20 Years of Practical Business Wisdom from the Trenches*. With his title covering all the bases, the subtitle shifted from selling the book to selling the author—traditionally what the bio has to do.

Similarly, *The 4-Hour Workweek*'s subtitle—*Escape 9-5, Live Anywhere, and Join the New Rich*—can go from piquing your interest to painting a tantalizing vision of the life you could have…if only you read this book. Because Tim Ferris did such a great job with the main title, the subtitle could provoke an even deeper emotional response, vs. having to finish doing the title's job in the first place.

A FINAL WORD ON THE 5 Cs

> *"Artists who seek perfection in everything are those who cannot attain it in anything."*
> ~ EUGÈNE DELACROIX

I'll share a bit of my father's hard-earned wisdom as an engineer with you: "Any time you solve one problem, you create another. The question is: is it worth it?"

Sometimes you can make your title easier to remember, but at the sacrifice of communicating what it's about. Sometimes you can set up your title for an entire series of business books, at the expense of any of the titles being interesting.

When in doubt, err on the side of clarity.

If your title is interesting but obscure (*Getting Naked*, *The E-Myth*), unless you have great marketing to fall back on, you won't enjoy the success you could have otherwise. If you have a specific marketing strategy that does not rely on the strength of your title, then you can afford to be weird, silly, or mysterious. Just keep in mind that the harder it is to grab your reader's attention…well, the harder it will be to grab their attention.

Don't kill yourself trying to create the best title in the history of mankind. If all else fails, just call your book what it is.

SOUND BITE SUMMARY

+ Your title must catch your reader's eye.

+ A *great* title can sell the book all by itself.

+ Some books are successful in spite of their titles—not because of them.

+ Be clear.

+ Don't sacrifice clarity to be clever.

+ If all else fails: just call your book what it is.

10

WHAT ELSE DO I NEED TO KNOW?

"Great writers are not born great. They are coaxed, coached, ghostwritten,
rewritten, edited, proofed, publicized, and published into greatness."

~ ROBERTA EDGAR

MOST PEOPLE SEE CARS as complicated machines. With so many moving parts and intricate systems, no one but grease monkeys truly knows what's going on under the hood.

Books, by contrast, seem simple: ink, paper, done.

Of course, you go through an arduous, painstaking process—fighting the Critic, wooing the Muse, writing and rewriting, sifting through your stories and ideas, and chaining yourself to your desk until you finally craft your masterpiece. After going through all that, you just want to pass it through spellcheck and hit print.

Alas and alack, my friend—your journey has just begun.

Unless you have been exposed to publishing, you are probably unaware of the rest of the process that goes into creating a physical product, much less what it takes to ultimately get it into the hands of your reader. Editing and typesetting; cover design and blurbs; publishers vs. self-publishing; printing and promotion—there is still work to do.

EDITING AND PROOFREADING

"Be careful about reading health books. You may die of a misprint."
~ MARKUS HERZ

Even when you're finished with your manuscript, you still don't have a finished manuscript.

Every author needs an editor. It's a fact of life.

I'm not talking about someone to make sure you spelled all your words right. I'm not talking about a writing coach to help you "punch up" your sentences. I mean a book professional who can objectively evaluate your manuscript, able to put their finger on what it needs to achieve its full potential.

You can wait until you're entirely finished before you hire someone to review it. Even better, you can hire them before you do your revisions so you can incorporate their suggestions early on, before you get too attached to one idea. Or you can hire them before you even begin, as a developmental editor. (Best of all, hire a ghostwriter.)

Regardless at what stage you seek professional help, be prepared for a good editor to challenge your ideas. They will tell you to change something and you will resist. After all, this is your baby, and nobody wants to hear they have an ugly baby.[1]

But if you want your baby to win a beauty pageant, you need to hear what your editor has to say.

Throughout this book, I have told you stories about how I work with authors to make their books better. Sometimes, my suggestions are

---

[1] Coincidentally, a day after drafting this section, I was in an online conversation with the legendary Tom Peters. He tweeted, "I can edit a draft 10–20 times but still DESPERATELY NEED outside eyeballs." If the management guru of the century needs outside help, then we all do.

minor—to rearrange some of their material to establish their authority upfront. Sometimes, my suggestions are major—writing a completely different book than the one they had in mind. Whether they implement my suggestions or not, the ideas I put forward make them think about their book from a completely new angle. Working together, we arrive at a stronger, better book than they would have written without some professional perspective.

If you go the traditional publishing route, your publisher will probably provide some level of editorial services (or at least feedback) as part of your contract. Even so, I still suggest hiring an independent editor of your own choice to help you make your book the very best it can be before sending it on to your publisher.

For one, if your manuscript requires substantial revision, your publisher is going to send it back to you with instructions on what to rewrite. So, you're going to be stuck doing the heavy lifting anyway. Better to have those things spotted and addressed by an editor with whom you work one-on-one.

Two, publishers' editors work for the publisher; that is, the publisher is their client. Their editor is going to be looking out for the best interests of the publisher, which are not always the same as yours. If you hire your own editor, then you are the client: they will be looking out for your best interests, which are not always the same as the publisher's.

Three, working directly with your own editor will probably result in a book that comes closer to your vision, rather than working with an editor who only has so many hours to devote to your manuscript—one of perhaps a dozen that they are working on at any one time.

(Of course, all of this advice hinges on you finding and qualifying a great editor in the first place. Do that.)

Your independent editor may or may not include proofreading as part of their services. However, a publisher will almost assuredly include proofreading as part of their contract. Even if they do, hire your own proofreader.

I have never seen a proofreader who could catch all the errors in a manuscript. My proofreader, Michael LaRocca, may be one, but I always proofread everything before I send it on to him, so he's never had the chance to prove me wrong. At the major publishing houses, they regularly use two, three, or even four proofreaders on a single manuscript (but don't count on it with your book). It is in your best interest to hire your own. That way, most of the errors will already be gone by the time your publisher's proofreader goes through it, letting them catch the rest.[2]

In fact, bestselling business author Tom Peters has hired his own editors and fact-checkers for his books since 1993—despite the ample resources I'm sure his publishers have made available to his projects.

The father of business books set the standard. Live up to it.

PRINTING VS. POD AND SELF-PUBLISHING VS. PUBLISHING

> *"How should you like to grow up a clever man, and write books, eh?"*
>
> *"I think I would rather read them, sir," replied Oliver.*
>
> *"What! wouldn't you like to be a book-writer?" said the old gentleman.*
>
> *Oliver considered a little while; and at last said he should think it would be a much better thing to be a book-seller; upon which the old gentleman laughed heartily, and declared he had said a very good thing.*
>
> ~ CHARLES DICKENS, *OLIVER TWIST*

Only after talking through everything that it takes to create a great business book does it make sense to talk about how to publish your work.

For the past century, the norm was for the author to write their manuscript and send it to a publisher. The process was straightforward: either your work was accepted and published (i.e., formatted, edited,

---

[2] But keep in mind that even with four proofreaders going through a book, it's nigh impossible to reach absolute zero. Some errors inevitably slip through the cracks. A handful of typos in a full-length manuscript is normal and acceptable.

typeset, proofread, etc.) or it wasn't. With few exceptions, it was all or nothing.

Today, the landscape has drastically changed. There are dozens of ways to distribute your work.

But let me simplify it for you. It really boils down to just two options:

1. Find a traditional publisher (what some would refer to as a "real publisher")
2. Do it yourself

There are very good reasons to go for one or the other.

A traditional publisher does not take a dime from you (and most traditional literary agents don't either). These entities make their money from the royalties of your book; their customer is the buyer. A traditional publisher will front the money it takes to do the editing, design, and production of your book, and then place your book in the main distribution channels. Depending on the probability of your success, they will invest additional money to market and promote your book. (But don't count on it. These days, many publishers follow the 80/20 rule: they spend 80% of their promotional money on the top 20% of their book lists.) This means you don't have to manage everything else. You write your book; they take care of the rest.

One disadvantage is the amount of time it takes between signing with a publisher until your book is actually released (often six to eighteen months). Another is that you give away most of the control of your book. The publisher is, in effect, buying certain rights to your intellectual property so they can sell it. By necessity, you cede an enormous degree of control.

The alternative is to do it yourself. If you do, you are ultimately responsible for the entire process of turning your words into a marketable product. You can hire some companies to do much of this on your behalf to whatever degree you choose, from outsourcing certain functions to individual professionals all the way to paying a company to do everything on your behalf. With self-publishing companies, keep in mind that they make their money from you, their customer (though some also take additional royalties from sales of your book). They leave the decision of how professional and how well-packaged your book is up to you. The good ones care about how well you serve your market, but even for them, how many copies you sell is secondary. Their profit comes from your pocket.

Of course, you have the distinct advantage of being in complete control of everything, from cover design to what texture of paper to how many copies you print. Too, you don't have to wait for decision-makers in New York to put your book through their process. You can have a book in your hands in a few weeks instead of several months.

If you do self-publish, then you have to wade through your printing options, which basically boil down to this: you get a discount for buying in bulk. If you want to print five thousand copies, you can find an offset printer who has the printing press to do this cost effectively. While a hefty upfront investment, you get more bang for your buck. If you want to print just a few hundred, you can find a smaller printer with the setup to do these "small" print runs. Although the cost per book will be higher, the upfront cost to print hundreds of books is more manageable than printing thousands.

On the extreme end of the scale, you can use a print-on-demand service. These services print one book at a time as the orders come in (ergo, "print-on-demand"). As you may imagine, it is expensive to print just one book, eating into your book royalties. Depending on your setup, though, this could cut your upfront costs to nearly zero. That way, your customers pay all the printing costs when they order the book online.

But the costs per book versus royalties and all other financial considerations are moot in the long run because…

BOOKS DON'T MAKE A BUCK

"I wrote the book to sell the game."
~ ROBERT KIYOSAKI ON HIS BESTSELLER *RICH DAD, POOR DAD*

You should go into this knowing full well that your book will not earn you a lot of money. In fact, it probably won't make any.

The ugly truth is that most business books never break even. The author invests more time and money than they ever make back from the sale of the copies. Add to that the opportunity costs of writing the book—that is, the value of their time they could have spent elsewhere—and some begin to wonder if there is any tangible benefit from writing a business book.

There are some exceptions. Some business authors' books hit the market just right (or, more likely, have a great marketing strategy behind them) and sell a million copies. Even earning two dollars a copy, those authors pocketed at least $2 million. But if you look at those authors, you will often find that they were making a lot of money to begin with. Their book's royalties are just the icing on the cake.

Marketing consultancy Wellesley Hills Group conducted a survey of 200 business authors. In an interview with *BusinessWeek*, the CEO said,

> *The vast majority of the authors we surveyed—96 percent—said they did realize a significant positive impact on their businesses from writing a book and would recommend the practice.*

The primary benefits were not book sales, but rather indirect benefits, such as "generating more leads, closing more deals, charging higher fees, and getting better speaking engagements."

Not every business book is an expert book and not every business author is a business owner. Some business books are works of love whose authors never intended for them to offer any return on their investment of time and money—and yet those authors still reap similar rewards. Take Marc Levinson's example from writing *The Box*, an engrossing history of the metal shipping container. (Yes, engrossing.) In the preface to the paperback edition, he wrote:

> *Early on in my work…I would proudly tell [people] I was writing a history of the shipping container. The result was invariably stunned silence…Eventually, I stopped talking about the book altogether…The*

response to the book's publication in the spring of 2006, then, caught me by surprise…[The] invitations began to arrive. In New York, I shared a platform with architects using containers to design office buildings and portents. In Genoa, I spoke alongside an entrepreneur who turned containers into temporary art galleries, while in Santa Barbara, California, the local museum joined forces with a university to [address] ramifications of the container I have never considered…

Even with a subject as seemingly boring as metal boxes and transportation, a book propelled an author to become an expert speaker and consultant—even though the author had no intention of becoming such.

That is the power of a book and its return on the author's investment.

I tell you this so that you go forward with your project with accurate expectations. You will not get rich from sales of your books. If you invest the money in a good editor, proofreader, cover designer, interior designer, and any other service providers you may need, you may not break even unless you sell several thousand copies.

But just one new client or opportunity may more than make it more than worth it. While I certainly hope *The Business Book Bible* is a commercial success, just one new ghostwriting client will pay for whatever I invest many times over.

In one sense, your book is a product in and of itself. As we have thoroughly discussed, it should satisfy a market need and deliver real value to your reader. At the same time, it is an incredibly powerful marketing tool. You should not expect any serious financial return; its benefit comes from it selling you and/or your company, your other products, and your subsequent books.

Writing a business book is just good business.

PUBLISHING PROFIT

"No man but a blockhead ever wrote, except for money."
~ SAMUEL JOHNSON

So how much money could you expect to make? Let's do some simple math.

A typical book might cost $2.49 per copy to print. That does not include whatever costs were spent on cover design, interior layout, ghostwriting, proofreading, etc. That is the direct cost to physically produce one book after everything has been designed.

Of course, that price widely varies depending on how you print. In general, the simpler your book is and the more you print in bulk, the cheaper it is per copy. But two-and-a-half bucks is a decent number to work with. Let's also say that your book retails for $19.95. The following table breaks down how a book moves through the publishing supply chain, and how much money is made at each step. (Just to be clear: the "sells at" price at one step is the "cost" price of the next step.)

A book begins with the publisher (if you self-publish, then this is you); the publisher sells the book to the wholesaler; the wholesaler sells the book either to a distributor or, in some cases, directly to the retail bookstore or bookseller. In most cases, the author does not receive any money until after the bookseller sells the book to the final customer.

Cost and Sell Price Per Book in Publishing Distribution

	Cost	(% of retail)	Sells at	(% of retail)	Gross profit
Publisher	$2.49	(12%)	$11.57	(58%)	$9.08
Wholesaler	$11.57	(58%)	$12.97[3]–$13.97	(65%–70%)	$1.40–$2.40
Distributor	$12.97	(65%)	$13.97	(70%)	$1.00
Bookseller	$13.97	(70%)	$19.95	(100%)	$5.99
Author	n/a		n/a		$2.49 (or ~20% of publisher gross)

©2003 Claudia Suzanne. Used and revised with permission.

---

[3] If a distributor is involved; otherwise, the wholesaler sells directly to the bookseller.

Keep in mind what "gross profits" mean. That $9.08 the publisher earns has to cover the direct costs of editing, formatting, and design of the book (but not the printing; that's what $2.49 covers), not to mention the indirect costs of salaries, the office lease, trade shows, and everything else it takes to run a business. The same goes for the other middlemen: those gross profits have to cover distribution, shipping, sales commissions, and whatever else it takes to get your book from printer to reader.

A business book is generally considered a publishing success if it sells 5,000 copies. Unfortunately—and don't let this deter you—most business books sell fewer than that.

So if a "successful" business book sells 5,000 copies and your cut is $2.49 per copy, then the profit from a successful book is a whopping $12,450. You could buy a decent used car for that or remodel your bathroom, but it is a far cry from retiring. You can't even live for a year on that.

If you self-publish and pocket the difference, optimistically your gross might be $45,400. That would cover a good editor and the other professionals it would take to design and produce your book…but not much else.

Now, your book may be different. You might sell a hundred thousand copies. Over the course of a few years, you might even sell a million. But the odds are against you, and I'm not a gambling man.

SOUND BITE SUMMARY

+ Everyone needs an editor. Period.

+ Writing your manuscript is only one part of publishing a book.

+ Regardless of whether you have a publisher or self-publish, thoroughly understand what it takes to publish a book.

+ Hire your own editor and proofreader, even if you have a publisher.

✦ Business authors don't count on their book sales; they count on what their book sells.

✦ Writing a business book is good business.

✦ Don't expect your book to make a profit.

11

Think Like a
Publisher

*"I learned early that class is universally admired.
Almost any fault, sin, or crime is considered more
leniently if there's a touch of class involved."*

~ Frank Abagnale, *Catch Me If You Can*

Here's the number one secret to self-publishing success: don't let it look like a self-published book.

Years ago, your responsibility as the author ended with having your words on paper. You wouldn't need to read my advice in this section unless you self-published. But today, even traditionally published authors have to be familiar with what it takes to design and create the final product.

With the advent of ebooks, ereaders, and other media vying for consumers' attention, the publishing industry's profits have been squeezed. ("Crushed" is more like it.) They just don't have the money to "do it right" as often as they used to. Ergo, more of the work, responsibility, and management is being pushed onto the author.

In both scenarios, business authors must take it upon themselves to understand the whole process. I must share a couple of post-writing tips with you so that you don't muck it up.

THE PACKAGING

"All buying decisions are made on the illustration, design, and the sales copy on the outside of the book. Yes, packaging is everything."
~ DAN POYNTER, *WRITING NONFICTION*

"Anyone who says that you can't judge a book by its cover has never met the buyer from Barnes & Noble."
~ TERRI LONIER, WORKING SOLO

You have to keep two different people in mind while working on your book: the reader and the buyer.

The reader is the person we have talked about throughout this book: the person for whom you write. The buyer is not literally the person who buys your book, but rather the gatekeeper to your reader.

Traditionally, the buyer was the representative at a company who decided whether to allocate shelf space to a particular book. If it was a major chain, they were literally called "the buyer"; if an independent bookstore, probably the owner or manager. Even in tiny bookshops, no one had the time to read all the new books released. These gatekeepers made their choices largely on the information provided by the publisher's salesperson. The most powerful tool in the salesperson's toolkit was the cover.

If the cover looked professionally designed and immediately caught their eye, the same would probably be true with their patrons. If the blurbs and sales copy were equally impressive, then the book stood a good chance of finding a temporary home on their shelves.

(Of course, having a movie or famous person behind the book helped more. Writing a book may be a literary endeavor, but selling a book is purely business.)

These days there are dozens of other venues through which to distribute and sell your book besides strictly traditional bookstores. The thirteen-store L.A. clothier Kitson racked up $1.6 million in book sales alone in the same year the bookseller Borders went bankrupt. Corporate executives often buy business books in bulk for their entire division (or even company) without finishing the book themselves. In fact, I used to have a passive-aggressive boss who, when faced with an employee problem, would search for a book to address the problem, buy it, and then "gift" it to the employee.

In all these instances, the gatekeeper made their purchasing decision on the strength of the cover and the benefits made in the sales copy—not on whether the book was actually worth reading. My point is that when you get ready to design the packaging of your book—its cover, the spine, the back cover/dust jacket text, the interior design, the feel of the pages, the blurbs—you want to create it so that it will persuade people to *buy* your book, which is different from persuading people to *read* your book.

But let me sound a note of caution. While writing this, I bought a book on America's economic recovery. (With degrees in economics and economic development, I am interested in that kind of thing.) The cover looked appealing and was professionally done, the typesetting looked fine, and the author was legitimate. It had the credentials of being a good book. But it only took me a couple of short chapters before I realized I had been gypped: at least half of the book was about one specific niche industry—which the author described in excruciating detail. I put the book down in disgust. I had been suckered in. The author had won me over as a buyer, but had completely lost me as a reader. Your book's packaging should appeal to more than just your ideal reader—but neither can it break your promise to the reader to deliver on the promise you implicitly make with the packaging.

When you write your book, write it for the reader; when you package your book, package it for the buyer.

COVER DESIGN

"Always use trained professionals to produce your cover.
A bad cover can cost you a hundred times the money
you think you saved in the form of lost sales."
— DAWSON CHURCH

We judge books by their covers.

They tell us not to. They warn us of all we are missing. They wag their finger and say, "Tsk, tsk." They are morally and intellectually superior to us illiterate peons who gravitate to "popular" books with mass-market appeal. They tell us to eat cake.

But when I walk into a Barnes and Noble, faced with some two hundred thousand titles, how else can I figure out which books are worthy of my attention and which I should ignore? With a gazillion books on Amazon, what am I supposed to do? Read the description of each and every book that my search returns?

Not.

Your book cover has a singular but incredibly important job: to get your buyer's attention. It exists for no other purpose.

It does not need to introduce your buyer to your concepts and material. It does not need to promote you, the author. It does not need to invoke a sense of wonderment or transport them to another place. All it needs to do is get their attention.

Once it snags their eye, then everything else takes over. They read the title. If you followed my advice, the title should quickly turn them on or off—they should immediately be able to tell if the book applies to their situation. If it does, they will investigate further by picking up the book or clicking through to the about page. They'll read the back cover and blurbs. They'll glance through the table of contents. They may even read a page or two.

As I shared earlier, in *Writing Nonfiction* Dan Poynter shared a study that found a bookstore browser spends an average of eight seconds looking at the front cover and a whopping fifteen seconds looking at the back. This means you have less than thirty seconds to make a great impression—if they even pick up your book in the first place.

It all begins with a great cover.

So, then, what does a great business book cover look like?

First, let's say what business covers don't look like: they don't look like everything else that's *not* a business book. When you walk into a bookstore, even without looking at the signs, you can guess what section you're in just by looking at the covers. Romance novels always have Fabio holding a helpless damsel in his arms. Cookbooks have some kind of food in some kind of arrangement on some kind of surface. History books usually feature a photograph, usually in sepia or black and white.

From across the store, though—too far away to make out the title— you can make out the business section: bright, contrasting colors, often in bands; few pictures; most of them simply have words. You can spot a business book from a mile away.

At least, that's what business books look like nowadays. That look has changed over time. In fact, you can almost guess in what decade a book was released just from its design. The original cover of *In Search of Excellence* has a black background and dark gold lettering—very masculine and very 80s. By the early 90s, covers had white backgrounds with horrible colors, like the mauve and mint green of the original print run of *7 Habits*, and copious amounts of text. Around the turn of the millennium, designers downplayed the amount of text, focusing on bright, solid backgrounds and blocky text, like the iconic cover of *Good to Great*.

The cover design of your book dates your book, just as surely as the design of a house, suit, or car dates it. If you want your book to look like it was published this year, then you need to hire a designer who does their homework and keeps up with the latest developments in this niche field.

One thing that has remained constant is the superfluity of images. Business readers are looking for solutions to their problems, and they need a signal from your book that you have it. "A picture is worth a thousand words," but this seems to be the one place in the universe where a picture actually gets in the way of communicating.

This is not a set-in-stone rule. There are rare cases of designers artfully incorporating an image that actually enhances the cover. *Freakonomics* and *Made to Stick* are two great examples. Plenty of business books have images tastefully incorporated into their design, such as *The Art of the Sale* or *The 4-Hour Workweek*, that do a fine job of conveying the mood of the book, but those images were not really necessary.

Then there are some books whose use of images does not make the book's intent any clearer than it would have been without it. It took me some time to realize that the picture on *The Art of the Start* was a match being struck. I still don't understand the marbles on the cover of *Outliers*. I get that one marble is separated, hence an "outlying" marble… but I still don't get it.

Then, too, there is the option to use your own picture. This is effective only if you have a recognizable face. It makes sense when Warren Buffet, Donald Trump, or Richard Branson puts their picture on the cover. Their mug is one of the most valuable marketing tools they have. It does not make much sense for people who are not somewhat famous or recognizable. What's the point? That you get to see yourself? Mirrors are cheaper.

Here is the main exception to the rule: when your picture adds some sort of context to the title. For example, a book on how to lead a board of directors with a picture of the female author on the cover; a woman on the board of directors tells you the book will be far different from a similar book with a rich white guy on the cover. *It's Your Ship* features the author in his dress uniform standing at the prow of a US destroyer; his picture adds additional context for the title of the book and the experience of the author.

Creating a great cover begins with these core choices. These are some of the basic elements. The rest of them, though, go deep into the realm of designer territory. Typesetting, font choice, font color, font size, font placement, background, the placement of the author's name, the inclusion of a blurb, the coating of the cover, the texture of the letters—there are hundreds of trifling details that must all work in tandem to convey the right message to your reader.

But as Michelangelo said, "Trifles make perfection, and perfection is no trifle."

TYPESETTING

"Good design, when done well, becomes invisible. It's only when it's done poorly that we notice it."

~ JARED SPOOL

You want a beautiful cover for your book, of course.

If you're like most self-published authors—and I say "self-published" because most traditionally published authors get little say in the design of their book's cover—you will belabor over the design, layout, and color of the cover. You want it to look perfect.

But it does not occur to many people to spend the same kind of time on the inside of their book.

I had a client who chose to go the self-publishing route. They hired an inexpensive cover designer, and did not hire an interior designer or typesetter at all. While the content of their book is brilliant (their ghostwriter did an excellent job, I must say), you can tell that it was laid out in Microsoft Word.

If you know anything about publishing, you should be blanching at the thought. It's like going into a retailer with a flier taped to the front doors that just came off the low-on-toner printer in the back office. It looks amateurish, immature, and cheap. It sticks out so much because we're used to professionally designed layouts. The standard displays of a retail store look "just so." A notice printed off ten minutes ago looks tacky.

The same is true for the layout of your book. Since we, the general public, have bought books from professional publishers for years, we know what a professionally laid out book looks like. Or, more accurately, we know what a professionally laid out book doesn't look like. When you open a book that has not been professionally typeset, you may not be able to point out exactly what's wrong, but it *feels* wrong.

It lacks polish, grace, and style.

There are "rivers" running through the text that visually distract you. The font choice puts you in the wrong frame of mind. (Yes, they can do that. It's the original subliminal marketing tactic.) The length of each line is off, either so long that you lose your place or so short that the read feels choppy. Then, of course, what about bullets, italicized passages, widows and orphans, drop capitals, kerning, and the other myriad invisible elements that we have unconsciously come to love and expect? The quote that opened this section applies to interior design: when done well, it becomes invisible. It's only when it's done poorly that we notice it.

Do it right. Go pro. Get a typesetter.

THE BACK COVER/DUST JACKET

"There is much to discover that's not on the back cover!"
~ E.A. BUCCHIANERI

In an ideal world, your cover would catch a bookstore browser's eye and they would decide to buy your book based just on the title. But as I pointed out earlier, we make subconscious decisions first, and then consciously look for rational reasons to justify that decision. Even if your would-be reader has already decided to buy your book, you need to give them reasons to feel good about their decision. If they are still on the fence, then you need to finish selling your work.

Your back cover copy and bio need to do two things[1]:

✦ finish convincing the browser that this is the book they have been looking for; that is, interest and intrigue them

---

[1] Please believe this advice applies equally to online "about" pages and "about the author" sections.

✦ set the stage for you to present your ideas inside the book; that is, earn their trust and respect

Think of it this way: if your book were a movie, the cover and cover copy would be the movie trailer. A movie trailer does not tell you the whole story. It does not give you the moral lessons you will learn by watching the movie. Sometimes it does not even perfectly mirror the movie (i.e., splicing some scenes together to make a better punch line or to dramatize a moment). In fact, some trailers are far better than the movies themselves.

Movies don't sell theater tickets; trailers do.

Just like editing, cover design, and the like, you should get a professional copywriter to help you write your back cover copy. If you have a publishing contract, they will have one for you. Either way, you should still draft your own. One, this will help you be more clear in the marketing and advertising you do for your book (which you will have to do even if you have a publisher). Two, the copywriter will not likely be familiar with your industry, your business, or even your concept. In fact, they may not even read your manuscript, much less extract the salient value for your reader. You know your material better than anyone else, so help these other professionals help you.

When you sit down to draft your back cover copy, go back to the exercise on identifying your one reader and the exercise on writing a great title. What benefits did you identify? What problems are they looking to solve? What words would catch their attention? What one thing could you ask or say that would send a clear signal to them that you know exactly where they are and what they need? The latter will be your headline on the back. The answers to your other questions will form the focus of the subsequent paragraphs.

But, of course, you don't want to simply tell people. You want to entice them—to whet their appetite enough that they cannot wait to buy your book and read it. Could you use a story? A metaphor so they quickly see the parallels? Some impressive or incredible yet believable statistic that makes them want to know more? Set them up so they can see the tangible benefit at the end of the journey, but leave blank the roadmap to get there.

This also applies to hardcovers with dust jackets. The difference is that the back is given entirely over to blurbs, while the sales copy and author bio is put on the inside flaps.

AUTHOR BIOS

> *"Never question the relevance of truth, but always*
> *question the truth of relevance."*
> ~ CRAIG BRUCE

Recall the story from chapter six of Joshua Bell playing his violin in the subway station. People rushed past, not realizing the world-class talent they brushed up against. They were not prepared to pay attention to this maestro because they did not have the proper context through which to experience it.

You have to provide people a frame in which to place the expertise you provide. Without educating them on who and what you are, they may never appreciate the genius that is at their fingertips.

While it may seem that an author's bio is just a self-serving chance to brag on themselves, it actually serves as an integral part of the product's—that is, the book's—packaging. If the author does not have any relevant experience and lackluster credentials, then they do not inspire much confidence in their advice and information. Thousands of crackpots out there have ideas they believe to be profound and life changing. Everyone has run across two or three of these people, if not a dozen. They believe themselves to be brilliant and they believe their book worthy of your hard-earned dollars.

Your bio is your chance to separate yourself from the herd. This is where you can present your qualifications to indicate that respectable people have vetted you and your ideas. This is where you persuade your would-be reader that you know your stuff. The one and only thing you're doing here is convincing them that you are impressively credible: they can trust you and, therefore, can trust what your book says. Ergo, the only credentials relevant in your bio are the ones relevant to your book.

Having the world's largest collection of aglets will not help your reader respect your insights on agribusiness; the fact that you have a PhD in agriculture would. Being a business owner may be too generic to include, but being the founder of a multimillion dollar manufacturer definitely qualifies for inclusion.

If you have a conferred title of any kind, use it. The more majestic it sounds, the better. Richard Branson is the legendary figure he is, but I would still always use his title of Sir (as many media releases do). If you were a judge or mayor, always use "The Honorable..." If you were an ambassador, always use "His Excellency..." If you served in the military, always use your rank: Sgt., Lt. Col., Commander.

Include other titles and education-related credentials if they are relevant to your book and/or your audience. If your book is related to urban development or small business growth, then include the fact that you are a certified economic developer. Many casual browsers may not understand the significance of that, but those who do will regard you a bit more.

For the market you're writing for (the general business trade audience), a bachelor's degree is somewhat expected. As such, to include a reference to a bachelor's actually weakens your authority. Like having too long of a bio, it makes you look like you're trying to convince the reader, versus confidently presenting your impressive credentials. A master's degree falls somewhere between a bachelor's and doctorate. If your degree is relevant to your book, then refer to your "master's in _____." Otherwise, leave the reference out. Referencing a master's in accounting when your book is about software development still makes it look like you're trying too hard.

Referencing a client is a great way to convey a wealth of information in just a word. When I tell people about my client Dr. Karin Stumpf's book, I always say, "She worked on an aspect of the merger between Chrysler and Mercedes-Benz." That immediately says that she's serious, she works in high business circles, her billion-dollar clients have vetted her, and she knows what she's doing.

List accomplishments or awards that can signal a lot of meaning. If you won any kind of relevant and "real" award or recognition (versus something like "voted most likely to succeed"), name it. Here, we find an exception to the relevance rule: if you won a Nobel Prize for anything, say so. An award like that is so prestigious that it doesn't matter how relevant it is to your book's topic.

Numbers carry an important weight. You can hide behind words and rewrite a narrative to suit the point of your story. It's harder to hide behind numbers. Have you given over one hundred speeches? Have you written five nonfiction books? Have you personally coached three dozen executives? Do you have a seven-figure consultancy? Are you responsible for doubling your client's business? Have you worked with ten of the *Fortune* 500? Specificity carries serious weight.

Your back cover copy needs to be intriguing; your bio needs to be informative. All together, your book's packaging has to be convincing.

BLURBS

> *"Just what the world needs…another business book!"*
> – US CUSTOMS AGENT, AS QUOTED BY JOSH KAUFMAN IN
> *THE PERSONAL MBA*

I trust a select few people when it comes to recommending business books.

I bought *The Art of the Sale* solely because the front cover featured a blurb by Tom Peters. The same goes for anything endorsed by Malcolm Gladwell and Daniel Pink. I've read their work, know how they think, and respect their judgment.

That's what a blurb does for your book. With just a sentence or two, plus a name and position, you can bypass all your buyer's hesitation and mistrust and get right down to business.

You do not have to be shy about asking for a blurb. It is something of a favor to you, but it is also a bit of a favor to the endorser. The more places their name appears, the more publicity and attention they get. Even if they are at the top of their game, they need additional momentum to stay there. If enough people see someone's name in enough places, they think, *Oh, I see this guy's name everywhere—he must be important.* It's a you-scratch-my-back-I'll-scratch-yours situation.

One of my clients asked me how many blurbs he should shoot for. I said, "Well, can you really have too many people saying good things about your book?" In the revised version of *The Sales Bible*, Jeffrey Gitomer has sixty blurbs between his cover, back cover, and front matter. You really can't have too many good endorsements—as long as the person's experience or position is somehow relevant to your book. Your uncle's endorsement of your book on how to be a successful street performer is worthless—unless, of course, he made a living performing in the French Quarter for a decade.

Most people are flattered to be asked to write a blurb. Begin with your contacts and extended network. If you want someone's endorsement and they are completely outside your network, don't be afraid to approach them directly. Simply (and sincerely) say how much you respect their opinion and how much you would appreciate their endorsement of your book.

Here's a publishing secret: the people who write blurbs rarely read the entire manuscript. If you go to Barnes and Noble and pull down all the books endorsed by the late Zig Ziglar, you would probably have a couple of shelves' worth. While Zig was a voracious reader, there's no way he had time to read all those books, write his own, and engage in all his other business ventures and projects. Like most reviewers, he read one or two sample chapters that gave him enough to know:

a. that the author was for real and had a "real" book

b. what the general gist of the book was

You and I do the same thing. Two chapters into a book, I have a good feel for where the author is going, whether what they say rings true, and whether they deserve my time and attention. The people who write blurbs usually stop there because they know enough. So, you do not have to wait until your book is finished to begin soliciting blurbs. You can begin as soon as you have just a couple of chapters polished enough to be impressive.

What an endorser says is far less important than who they are. You can pay people in Elbonia to write blurbs for your book...but so can everyone else. To impress your reader, you need blurbs that come with a prominent title or position. I could offer a dynamic, jaw-dropping blurb of a friend's fantasy novel that would count for nil because, in that world, I'm nobody. If, on the other hand, George R.R. Martin of *Game of Thrones* fame simply wrote, "Buy this book," it would fly off the shelves.

When you begin to get responses back, rank them by how impressive of a person they are (i.e., Richard Branson) or how impressive of a position they have (i.e., CEO of Random House). You may be tempted to rank someone who has more clout in your particular industry or niche over someone who is more famous in general. For instance, on a book about writing books, the CEO of Random House would be more relevant than Richard Branson. Don't lose sight of the forest for the trees: if someone famous endorses your book—even if they have nothing at all to do with your book's topic—lead off with them. I don't care if your book addresses the shortcomings of CRM solutions: if Oprah endorses it, her name goes to the top of the list.

Now, let's talk about real estate.

You want to put your best blurb where it gets the most attention: the front cover. Depending on your cover design, you might have room for two. The next most valuable real estate is on the back of your book. List three or four blurbs here, even if you do not have a dust jacket. Without a dust jacket, that may leave you only a paragraph's worth of copy to talk about your book. That's okay. If you do it right, all the space those blurbs take up will be far more weighty than anything you could ever write.

Once you've exhausted the real estate on your cover, begin with the very first page of your book, starting with the best blurb you haven't used yet. Then, list them in descending order.

This arrangement puts your best foot forward, putting the most impressive blurbs in the highest-impact places. Once people get through the first page of endorsements, however, plenty of people will skim or even skip through the middle, but linger on the very last blurb. For that reason, choose one semi-prominent blurb (perhaps one that you would have started your second page with) and place it as the very last.

You want your roll call of glowing praise to end with a flourish, not a sputter.[2]

SOUND BITE SUMMARY

+ The #1 secret to self-publishing success: don't let it look like a self-published book.

+ The packaging sells the book.

+ Package your book so people will *buy* it. That's different than persuading them to *read* it.

+ Don't get cheap with your cover.

+ Your cover exists to get your reader's attention. That's it.

+ Go pro—get a typesetter.

---

[2] With this book, I was fortunate enough to have an all-star cast of blurb writers. All of them are impressive, accomplished business and publishing professionals in their own right. It was next to impossible to try to sort them according to the criteria I lay out there. Really, the order of my blurbs wasn't about who was more impressive but who had better name recognition.

- ✦ Your cover copy and author bio have to convince your reader that your book is worth their time and money.

- ✦ The right blurb can sell your book faster than anything else you could write.

Author's Note

---

*"My father was a man who loved his business. When he talked about it
I never felt that he regarded it as a venture for making money; it was an
art, to be practiced with imagination and only the best materials. He had
a passion for quality and had no patience with the second-rate; he never
went into a store looking for a bargain. He charged more for his product
because he made it with the best ingredients, and his company prospered."*
~ William Zinsser, *On Writing Well*

This quote captures the essence of my approach to business books. They aren't merely a marketing tool or an ego trip, but neither are they works of art with no practical application. They are artisanal products, made with the finest materials and offered in trade for something else just as valuable.

Civilization as we know it took off when farmers began producing enough surplus food so that not everyone had to be a hunter or gatherer. Instead of going into the field, some people could devote themselves to the skills needed to store the extra crops, like firing pottery or building granaries. Eventually, farmers created enough surplus to support larger communities, leading to even more types of specialized vocations: blacksmiths, artisans, musicians, scribes, priests, and poets.

The key concept that enabled all of this was trade: the farmer traded his crops and livestock to the potter for storage jugs, to the cooper for barrels, to the tanner for saddles, and to the chandler for candles so they could work at night.

But what about when the farmer didn't want the musical instrument the artisan made? The musician didn't trade with the farmer; he traded the flute to the tailor who had traded clothing to the farmer for food. At some point, some tradesmen specialized in brokering these transactions: not making goods but trading them for others so that everyone got what they wanted.

Eventually merchants realized they needed a better means of trading—a way to represent the value of goods and services so they wouldn't have to lug everything around with them. Precious commodities became the answer: salt, gold, and gems. Enough existed to become a practical means of exchange, but were still rare enough to be valuable. Today, we simply use currency.

I'm not leading up to suggesting what price tag to put on your book. You want something much more valuable than your reader's twenty dollars. You want their attention, admiration, goodwill, respect, and business. If you want to receive something of great value, you first have to create something of great value. If you want your business book to give you a great return on your investment of time and money, you need to make sure you're writing something worth reading.

If you offer a shoddy book to the world in trade…well, guess what you'll get in return?

But if you give the world a wonderful book, chock full of things people need and want to know, presented in a way that delights, entertains, and enthralls…well, you reap what you sow.

About the Author

Derek's love for business books began with a Brazilian missionary's tattered 1979 copy of *Quest for the Best*.

It was love at first read.

While his peers were reading the 90s' equivalent of *Twilight*, Derek was devouring books on economics, biographies, success stories, business management, entrepreneurship, and anything else business-related.

After high school, he earned a degree in economics from Louisiana Tech and then a master's in Latin American business and economic development from the University of Florida. His graduate thesis was based on his field research with Dominican loan sharks.

Derek's professional career experience includes being the administrator of a nonprofit that sheltered expecting and parenting teens. He was also the in-house business and marketing consultant for a $30 million company group, during which he assumed day-to-day operations of a $2 million company for months during a leadership crisis.

Ever the entrepreneur, he left conventional employment to start an IT services company with a coworker (still successfully in business). During the start-up phase, Derek supported his family by taking on copywriting projects. Once he realized he could make a living combining his two loves—business and writing—he decided to pursue a full-time career as a business writer.

Today, Derek works with leaders who are serious about making the world a better place through better business. He has worked with clients on five continents with topics spanning economics, leadership, sales, and international tax law. His authors work with and for SAP, the International Monetary Fund, DaimlerChrysler, Amazon, Microsoft, Walmart, and the Red Cross.

He grew up in Mayberry (a.k.a. Pitkin, Louisiana) and now lives with his wife and two children in Baton Rouge.

ACKNOWLEDGMENTS

"I love teamwork. I love the idea of everyone
rallying together to help me win."
~ Jarod Kintz, *A Zebra Is the Piano of the Animal Kingdom*

I AM INDEBTED TO A HOST OF PEOPLE for their support, encouragement, and help in putting together *The Business Book Bible*.

My wonderful wife, who patiently listened to my ideas and excitement, suggested great ideas, and believed in me when I didn't believe in myself.

Paul Bovino, Sally Collings, John Kador, Michael Slavin, and Claudia Suzanne, who provided sound advice and made this a better book.

My endorsers, who took the time to read this book and write such glowing testimonials.

My clients, who provided a wealth of incredible collaborative writing opportunities.

Michele DeFilippo and her team at 1106 Design, for patiently working with me on the cover and interior design to turn my digital manuscript into a "real" book.

Michael LaRocca, my incredible proofreader and secret weapon.

Lastly, my readers: thank you in advance for reading my work. I look forward to your thoughts and insights.

Miscellaneous
and Extraneous

This resource is designed to provide information on writing and editing business trade books. It is provided with the understanding that the author is not engaged in rendering legal, accounting, or other professional services. Such topics, as discussed herein, are for example or illustrative purposes only. If you need legal, financial, or other professional assistance, you should use the services of an appropriately qualified professional to receive specific advice.

It is not the purpose of this resource to reprint all the information that is otherwise available to authors and/or publishers, but to complement, amplify, and supplement other resources. You are urged to read all the available material and learn as much as you can about producing a successful business book and to tailor the information to your circumstances.

Every effort has been made to make this resource as complete and as accurate as possible. However, there may be mistakes, both typographical and in content. Therefore, this text should be used only as a general guide and not as the ultimate source of writing and publishing information. Furthermore, this resource contains information on writing and publishing that is current only up to the date of release.

The purpose of this resource is to educate and entertain. The author shall have neither liability nor responsibility to any person or entity with respect to any loss or damage caused, or alleged to have been caused, directly or indirectly, by the information contained herein.

If you do not wish to be bound by the above, you may return this resource to the author for a full refund.

Made in the USA
Columbia, SC
26 February 2019